ZION
A LIGHT IN THE DARKNESS

ALEXANDER B. MORRISON

DESERET BOOK COMPANY, SALT LAKE CITY, UTAH

This book is not an official publication of The Church of Jesus Christ of Latter-day Saints. No one asked me to write it. The views and ideas presented herein are my own and do not necessarily represent the position or view of the Church. I alone am responsible for errors or omissions in the text.

This book is dedicated to my dear eternal companion, Shirley, who is and ever will be a light and refuge for me.

Jenny Pedersen and Katherine Tanner typed, proofread, and corrected the manuscript with great skill and devotion. I am indebted to Michelle Arciaga for careful reading of chapter three, and to Stuart Reid and Carolyn Hyde for their encouragement.

Library of Congress Cataloging-in-Publication Data

Morrison, Alexander B.
Zion : a light in the darkness / Alexander B. Morrison.
p.   cm.
Includes bibliographical references and index.
ISBN 1-57345-260-2
1. Zion (Mormon Church)   2. Christian life—Mormon authors.
3. United States—Moral conditions.   I. Title.
BX8643.Z55M675   1997
248.4'8932—dc21   97-11004
                                                                      CIP

Printed in the United States of America

10   9   8   7   6   5   4   3   2   1   18961

CONTENTS

INTRODUCTION

Israel, Israel, God is calling,
Calling thee from lands of woe.
Babylon the great is falling;
God shall all her tow'rs o'er-throw.
Come to Zion, come to Zion
Ere his floods of anger flow.
Come to Zion, come to Zion
Ere his floods of anger flow.

(Hymns, no. 7)

One of the greatest blessings of Zion is that God intends it as a refuge for the righteous, a place of safety for those fleeing the wickedness of a world wallowing in sin, a beacon in the twilight of a darkening world. In every age, "men and women of faith and hope have dreamed of a Holy City, whose king is the Lord God Omnipotent . . . where peace is in every heart, where there is no fear nor want and all people are brothers and sisters, where faith and purity shine in every face."[1]

The theme and central message of this book is that we must build Zion if we are to stand against the wickedness of the world. Our society is becoming increasingly wicked and antagonistic toward the eternal principles taught by Jesus Christ. God-given institutions such as the family and community are under continuous attack from the forces of the adversary; and corruption, violence, venality, and vice abound. Ours

v

is a day when men "call evil good, and good evil" (Isaiah 5:20), a day when the righteous must "flee unto Zion for safety" (D&C 45:68). Confronted as we are with an ever-escalating tide of wickedness, we have but two alternatives: to succumb, slip into the slime of the world, and be led blindly away to destruction, or, to turn away from wickedness, become men and women of Christ, and accept fully our covenantal responsibilities—in short, to leave Babylon and come to Zion.

Please do not suppose that I suggest faithful Saints all over the world should "pull up stakes" and depart for the Rocky Mountains. Not at all! Our prophet-leaders have advised us to stay in our own communities, to build Zion in our own stakes and wards. This is a task that has become much easier through the inspired program of temple construction around the world, which has so blessed the Saints in the last quarter century. Leaving Babylon and coming to Zion should be thought of as symbolic—the process of turning away from the world, of becoming pure in heart, of striving to attain the paradise, which, though lost, may be found again if we fully consecrate ourselves to Christ and His cause.

The establishment of Zion is contingent upon the development of a people who have completely consecrated their lives to Christ. Unfortunately, as President Spencer W. Kimball pointed out, "to be shown the way is not necessarily to walk in it,"[2] and much remains for us to do before we qualify to receive the blessings and protection of Zion.

The need for our day is clear: we must prepare a people qualified to build "the New Jerusalem, a land of peace, a city of refuge, a place of safety for the saints of the Most High God; and the glory of the Lord shall be there, and the terror of the Lord also shall be there, insomuch that the wicked will not come unto it, and it shall be called Zion.

"And it shall come to pass among the wicked, that every

man that will not take his sword against his neighbor must needs flee unto Zion for safety. And there shall be gathered unto it out of every nation under heaven; and it shall be the only people that shall not be at war one with another" (D&C 45:66–69).

In commenting on that scripture and its meaning for our day, President John Taylor said: "We are gathered here for the express purpose of carrying out the purposes of God; the world, however, do not understand it. But I tell you what they will do, by-and-by. You will see them flocking to Zion by thousands and tens of thousands; and they will say, 'We don't know anything about your religion, we don't care much about religious matters, but you are honest and honorable, and upright and just, and you have a good, just and secure government, and we want to put ourselves under your protection, for we cannot feel safe anywhere else. But we must prepare ourselves; we have got to have the invigorating influence of the Spirit of God to permeate all of our organizations, all feeling that we are under the guidance and protection of the Almighty, every man in his place, and every man according to the order of the priesthood in which God has placed him."[3]

This book is an attempt to identify the steady erosion of the moral and ethical underpinnings of our society, helping us better prepare ourselves for times to come. More importantly, it also offers suggestions on how we might reverse the onslaught of an ominous, darkening future. It is divided into two parts. Part One, "Darkening Skies," presents a brief overview of the current status of the moral and spiritual health of American society. Part Two, "Rolling Back the Darkness," suggests some ways to combat the darkness that threatens to engulf us.

The information in Part One is stark and serious, a somber manifestation of the times in which we live. It will be alarming to some. To one who recently complained to me about that fact, I replied, "My only defense is that the information is true. I didn't make it up. I believe it is better to face up to reality than to deny it until it's too late to take much-needed remedial action. The information I present should be seen as a wake-up call, not an admission of defeat."

Given that these are indeed the last days long foreseen by God's prophets, we should perhaps not be surprised by turmoil and travail on all sides. There will be trying times and dark days ahead to be sure, but the Latter-day Saints, of all people, should retain and practice a basic optimism. President Gordon B. Hinckley is one of the most optimistic men I know. Recently, he invited all members of the Church "to stand on your feet and with a song in your heart move forward, living the gospel, loving the Lord, and building the kingdom. Together we shall stay the course and keep the faith, the Almighty being our strength."[4] At the April 1996 general conference of the Church, President Hinckley proclaimed: "We go forward, marching as an army with banners emblazoned with the everlasting truth. We are a cause that is militant for truth and goodness. . . . Everywhere we go we see great vitality in this work. There is enthusiasm wherever it is organized. It is the work of the Redeemer. It is the gospel of good news. It is something to be happy and excited about. . . . Stand for truth with enthusiasm and without fear."[5]

Our peace and safety in these troubled times can be found only in totally rejecting the wickedness of the world and by embracing and living the teachings of Christ. Elder Bruce R. McConkie taught: "Men in our time will never find peace, or safety, or salvation in the world. Wars and plagues and desolation shall continue to sweep the earth as with a flood.

"Crime and evil will increase; iniquity will abound; the love of men toward each other shall wax cold [see Matthew

24:12]. We need not look for a day when men of themselves shall usher in an age of righteousness.

"But those who turn to Christ, who believe his gospel, and join his church, and live his laws, and who thereby worship the Father in his holy name—such shall find peace and safety and salvation. In the world men shall have tribulation; in Christ they shall find peace (see John 16:33)."[6] The scriptures assure us that "if ye are prepared ye shall not fear" (D&C 38:30). If we "live his laws," as Elder McConkie advised, follow the counsel of the living prophets, and "stand in holy places" (D&C 45:32), taking unto ourselves "the whole armour of God," we *will* "be able to withstand in the evil day" (see Ephesians 6:13–18). Thus prepared, we shall not fear!

As you read the ensuing pages, do not despair. After all, "they that be with us are more than they that be with them" (2 Kings 6:14–17).

DARKENING SKIES

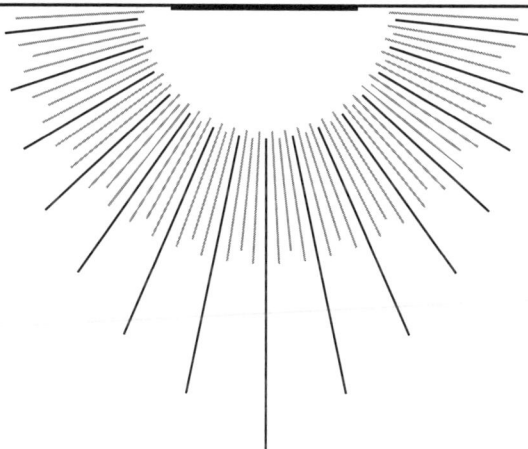

1

EVERY MAN WALKETH
IN HIS OWN WAY

In a defining article printed in *The Wall Street Journal*, William J. Bennett, former Secretary of Education in the government of the United States, noted that during the last three decades, from 1960–1990, the Gross Domestic Product (GDP) of the United States nearly tripled, and total social spending by all levels of government (measured in constant 1990 dollars) rose from $143 billion to $757 billion—more than a fivefold increase. At the same time, inflation-adjusted spending on education increased by 225 percent.[1]

On the surface it all sounds wonderful, the reflection of a golden age for the country, a time when America stands preeminent above all other nations in its efforts to attend to the social needs of its people. But don't be fooled by the figures; there is a dark and somber side to what is happening in our country, something Bennett describes as the "decline of America." These hard realities are illustrated by the following:[2]

◆ Violent crimes increased from 288,460 in 1960 (16.1 per 10,000 population) to 1,820,130 in 1990 (73.2 per 10,000 population). The rate of violent crimes in the U.S. is higher than in any other industrialized country: According to the U.S. Department of Justice, eight out of every ten Americans will be a victim of violent crime at least once in their lives.

♦ Nearly three of every four convicted criminals in the U.S. are not incarcerated, and fewer than one in ten serious crimes results in imprisonment. In 1990 the expected punishment for someone convicted of murder was 1.8 years in prison; for rape, the expected sentence was 60 days; for robbery, 23 days; for aggravated assault, only 6.4 days. The wages of sin, at least in terms of incarceration, don't amount to much!

♦ The percent of American children dependent on government welfare rose from 3.5 in 1960 to 11.9 in 1990. This more than threefold increase in welfare dependence directly reflects the alarming collapse of the family in the United States.

♦ The incidence of illegitimacy continues to escalate. In 1990, 65 percent of *all* births to African American women were illegitimate; in many inner-city communities, essentially all births are extramarital. Some observers have termed illegitimacy "the single most important social problem of our time—more important than crime, drugs, poverty, illiteracy, welfare, or homelessness because it drives everything else."[3] Federal government statistics for 1993 provide the following information on extramarital births in the United States:

- Over 1.2 million babies were born outside of marriage (31% of all births, up from 28% only three years previously).
- Only 48% of all nonmarital births were first births.
- Of mothers giving birth outside of marriage, 30% were teenagers, 35% ages 20–24, and 35% ages 25 and over.
- 82% of women born between 1954 and 1963 had premarital sex.

4

- The proportion of couples who marry between the conception of a child and its birth has declined. For white couples the figure fell from 61% in the 1960s to 34% in the 1980s; for African American couples it fell from 31% to 8% in the same period.
- Fewer babies are being placed for adoption. In the period between 1960 to 1973, one in five babies born outside of marriage to white women were placed for adoption; but in the 1980s only one in thirty such babies were placed for adoption.[4]

◆ Nearly one in four pregnancies now ends in abortion, with approximately 1.6 million abortions performed in 1990 and more than 28 million abortions during the years from 1973 (when the *Roe* v. *Wade* decision of the U.S. Supreme Court legalizing abortion was promulgated) to 1990.

According to a recent national survey, abortion is relatively common throughout a broad section of American women, including members of some religious groups considered by reason of their public positions to be opposed to it. About half of American women will have an abortion at some point in their lives.[5]

◆ The number of divorces in America has increased by nearly 200 percent in the last thirty years; only about 50 percent of U.S. marriages now are first-time marriages. The increase in divorces has led to an increase in the number of children directly affected by divorce.

The Plight of Our Children

The erosion occurring in the moral and ethical underpinnings so essential for the health and well-being of the nation is having a particularly deleterious effect on our children and adolescents. Indicators of the turmoil and tragedy that rip apart so many young lives include the following:

◆ The percent of children living in single-parent homes has more than tripled in the last three decades, to its current level of nearly 29 percent of all families with children. Approximately 90 percent of single-parent homes are fatherless. Some 1.3 million so-called "latchkey" children ages 5–14 are left to fend for themselves for much of the day. Unfortunately, without supervision, many of them get into trouble.

◆ The percent of mothers who work outside the home and who have a husband present in the home and children ages 6–17, increased from 28 percent in 1950 to 75 percent in 1993.[6] Statistics for the state of Utah, where Latter-day Saints make up the majority of the population, closely resemble those for the U.S. as a whole.

◆ According to the Children's Defense Fund,[7] every day in America:

- 3 children or youths under the age of 25 die from HIV infection (AIDS).
- 6 children or youths under the age of 20 commit suicide.
- 13 children or youths under the age of 20 are victims of homicide.
- 255 children or youths under age 18 are arrested for drug offenses.
- 318 children or youths under age 18 are arrested for alcohol-related offenses.
- 327 children or youths under age 18 are arrested for violent crimes.
- 2,217 students drop out of high school.

- 2,699 babies are born into poverty.
- 3,356 babies are born to unmarried mothers.

◆ The reported incidence of child abuse increased from 101 per 10,000 Americans in 1976 to 390 per 10,000 in 1990, an almost fourfold increase. Most experts agree that the majority of such cases are never reported to law enforcement authorities.

◆ The fastest growing segment of the criminal population in America is our nation's youth. Young people between the ages of thirteen and nineteen comprise only 12 percent of the U.S. population but account for more than 22 percent of violent crime. Juvenile crime rates have decreased overall during the last couple of years, but juvenile arrests for *violent* crimes are continuing to increase. According to the Federal Bureau of Investigation, the nearly quadrupling in juvenile arrests during the past three decades has involved not only the "disadvantaged minority youth in urban areas" but "all races, all social classes, and all lifestyles." Youths also are being arrested for violent crimes at younger ages. In 1982, for example, 390 teens aged thirteen to fifteen were arrested for murder. A decade later, this total had jumped to 740.[8] Many young criminals, who trust no one and live with no sense of the future, commit crimes of extreme violence for what seem to be unfathomably trivial reasons—the theft of sneakers, sweatpants, or lambskin coats, supposed insults, bragging rights, or perceived "props" (as in "proper respect"). Seemingly devoid of conscience, these vicious young people evince little or no regret for what they have done.

◆ Illicit drug use among teenagers rose an alarming 105

percent between 1992 and 1995, from 5.3 percent of those
surveyed in 1992 to 10.9 percent in 1995.[9]

◆ The number of unmarried teenagers getting pregnant has
nearly doubled in the past two decades. By the late 1980s,
nearly one unmarried teenage girl in ten got pregnant. The
number of abortions undergone by unmarried teenagers
(43.8 per thousand) is now approximately the same as the
number of live births (42.5 per thousand) in young women
of this age group, and in numerous inner-city settings there
are many more babies aborted than are carried to term.

◆ Since 1960 the rate of teenage suicide has more than
tripled, to a level where suicide is now the third leading
cause of death among adolescents, behind only motor vehicle accidents and all other accidents. The 2 April 1991
issue of *USA Today* reported that one-third of U.S. teenagers
say they have considered suicide, 15 percent have thought
seriously about it, and 6 percent have actually tried it.

◆ Sexually active youth are the norm, not the exception. Since
the 1960s, acceptance of sexual promiscuity has increased
in the United States and most other Western societies to the
point that having sexual relations outside of marriage is
widely portrayed as acceptable behavior in television
shows, movies, popular songs, and in newspaper and mag-
azine articles. This so-called "sexual revolution" has had a
marked impact on the behavior of young people. Many
more unmarried youth are sexually active today than ever
before in American history.

The extent of teenage sexual activity in America is well-
illustrated by the results of a study conducted in 1990–91 in
Forsyth County, North Carolina, by the Department of Public
Health Sciences at Bowman Gray School of Medicine.[10] The

Bowman Gray group surveyed 1,269 youth between the ages of twelve and nineteen—744 girls and 525 boys—representing a broad sampling of family incomes, although most described their family's lifestyle as "comfortable." Just over half (52 percent) of the respondents were African Americans, 48 percent were White.

The authors of the report concluded that "Forsyth County is experiencing an epidemic—teens having sex and having babies." The results of the study certainly substantiate such a conclusion: by the time they reach fifteen, half of all Black males surveyed, almost a third of the White males, a third of the Black females, and a quarter of the White females said they were having sex regularly. Before they turn twenty, from sixty to seventy percent of Forsyth County girls will have been pregnant at least once. Early sexual activity was found often to be part of a larger pattern of behavior—a lifestyle—that includes substance abuse. Fully sixty-five percent of young men who were heavy alcohol users were sexually active, as were forty-five percent of young women. Only about half as many of those who did *not* use alcohol were sexually active. Similar relationships were found between sexual activity and marijuana use. In other words, use of alcohol or marijuana is strongly associated with sexual activity in teenagers. The relationship between drug use and premarital sexual activity is not necessarily one of cause and effect; but the two are associated together as part of an overall lifestyle. Drug use is well-known to lower inhibitions, which may lead to increased extramarital sexual activity.

The authors of the Bowman Gray study concluded that the strongest compulsion to engage in early sex is what youth believe their friends, both boys and girls, expect of them. Sexually active youth think that having sex will give them

9

acceptance and status, and they believe most of their friends are sexually active.

I know of no reason to believe the results of the Bowman Gray study are not at least generally applicable elsewhere in the United States and in other Western countries. The findings indicate a crisis in teenage morality in this country, an epidemic of immorality that should concern us all and that threatens to morally destroy many in the next generation of Americans.

Information on how to respond in the Lord's way to the crisis currently engulfing the family is given in Part Two of this book (chapters 6–8).

2

THE DECLINE OF THE FAMILY

No aspect of the change that has so altered American society during the last thirty years is more foreboding than is family breakdown. Across the sweep of time and history, family disruption has been regarded everywhere as something that threatens a child's survival, health, and well-being. The reason is rooted in our biology. Colts, calves, and fawns are fully mobile and functional within a few hours of birth. But humans are different: the human child is born helpless and totally dependent on adults for food, shelter, and general care. Years of nurturing and protection are needed before an infant grows to physical independence. Similarly, years of loving, supportive interaction by caring adults are needed for a child to grow into a socially, emotionally, and spiritually competent adult.

In every culture and historical period, the social arrangement that has proved most successful in ensuring not only the physical survival and development of the child but also its social, emotional, and spiritual growth is the family unit—the child and its biological or adoptive mother and father. In a well-balanced and thoughtful essay in *The Atlantic Monthly* (April 1993), Barbara Defoe Whitehead pointed out that divorce or out-of-wedlock childbirth are transforming the lives of American children. She noted that in the post-World War II generation, more than eighty percent of children grew up in a family with two biological parents who were married to each other. By 1980 only fifty percent of children born in the U.S. could expect to spend their entire childhood in an intact family. "If current trends continue," Ms. Whitehead concluded, "less than half of all children born today will live continuously with their own mother and father throughout childhood. Most American children," she noted, "will spend several years in a single-parent family led by a mother. Some will eventually live in stepparent families, but because stepparent families are more likely to break up than intact [i.e., two-biological-parent] families, an increasing number of children will experience family breakup two or even three times during childhood." It requires little imagination to predict the social consequences of that kind of family instability and attendant trauma.

It has become conventional wisdom, accepted by many in universities and government, and eagerly embraced by Madison Avenue and Hollywood, that divorce is like a bad cold, with a phase of acute discomfort, followed by a short recovery period, and a rapid return to full health. The truth is tragically different. According to a growing body of well-documented evidence, children in families disrupted by divorce or out-of-wedlock birth do much worse than children in intact families on several measures of well-being. They include the following as documented in the article by Whitehead referred to previously, unless otherwise referenced:

◆ Children in single-parent families are two to three times as likely as children in two-parent families to have emotional and behavioral problems. Results from a California study conducted by Professor Judith Wallerstein,[1] show that five years after a divorce more than a third of the children

12

involved experienced moderate or severe depression. Whitehead notes that at ten years after divorce, a significant number of the now young men and women appeared to be troubled, drifting, and underachieving. At fifteen years, many of the children of divorce, by then in their thirties, were struggling to establish strong love relationships of their own. A higher than normal proportion of children from disrupted families have a harder time achieving intimacy in a relationship, forming a stable marriage, or even holding a steady job.

◆ Children in single-parent families are more likely to drop out of high school, to get pregnant as teenagers, to abuse drugs, and to be in trouble with the law. More than seventy percent of all juveniles in state reform institutions in the United States come from fatherless homes. The relationship between crime and one-parent families is so strong that it erases the relationship between race and crime and between low income and crime. Indeed, the single factor that best determines whether a young man will become a criminal is not his race, nor his economic status, but whether he has a father who lives with his mother and is married to her.

◆ Incidents of physical and sexual abuse of children are much higher in disrupted families than in families involving both biological parents. In a Canadian study conducted by Martin Daly and Margo Wilson at McMaster University in Hamilton, Ontario, preschool children in step-families were found to be forty times as likely as children in intact families to suffer physical or sexual abuse.[2]

◆ The father-child bond is severely, often irreparably damaged in families disrupted by divorce or illegitimacy. Close to half of such children have not seen their father at all in the past year. Many fathers have simply vanished.

13

Legislative action to find "deadbeat dads" and require them to accept their responsibilities toward their children can hardly be expected to replace what conscience has failed to voluntarily elicit. In the California study by Professor Wallerstein already alluded to, nearly three-fourths of the respondents, now young men and women, report having poor relationships with their absentee fathers.

The Family Is in Peril

Barbara Whitehead has stated that "survey after survey shows that Americans are less inclined than they were a generation ago to value sexual fidelity, lifelong marriage, and parenthood as worthwhile personal goals. Motherhood no longer defines adult womanhood; equally important is the fact that fatherhood has declined as a norm for men. In 1976 less than half as many fathers as in 1957 said that providing for children was a life goal. The proportion of working men who found marriage and children burdensome and restrictive more than doubled in the same period. Fewer than half of all adult Americans today regard the idea of sacrifice for others as a positive moral virtue."[3]

The conclusion to be reached from a recounting of this lamentable litany of selfishness and irresponsibility seems clear: the most important stabilizing influence in society, the family, is in dire peril. The family is being dramatically weakened and undermined, and too few people seem to care enough to do anything about it. A leading American academic expert agrees with that view. David Popenoe has said: "The American family is not simply changing: it is getting weaker. . . . Family decline drives some of our most urgent social problems. . . . The heart of the family problem lies in the steady breakup of the two-parent home. Most social

14

scientists who study the family have become much more, not less, pessimistic in recent years about the state of the American family."[4]

Where Have All the Fathers Gone?

In a recent intelligent and courageous book, David Blankenhorn has chronicled what he describes as the most dangerous social trend of our generation, fatherlessness.[5] He points out that more than half of American children will spend at least some of their childhood growing up without a father in the home, and that in a radical departure from virtually all of human history, responsible fatherhood is declining disastrously in our society. Fathers are increasingly viewed as expendable, irrelevant, and of no real value. Fatherlessness, Blankenhorn points out, is the engine driving our most urgent social problems, from crime to adolescent pregnancy to child abuse to domestic violence against women. Yet in the face of the alarming facts so carefully assembled by Blankenhorn, our society does little, or worse, glorifies the increasing "deculturation" of fatherhood. As a result, fatherhood is rapidly losing its four traditional roles: caregiver and protector, moral educator, head of family, and breadwinner.

The following table (Blankenhorn, 18, 227) illustrates the shrinking role of fatherhood in America.

Indicators of Fatherhood in America

	1960	1990
Percent of births outside marriage	5.3	28.0
Divorced males per 100,000 married males	27.4	112.5
Percent of children living apart from their fathers	17.5	36.3
Percent of children living with biological father and mother	80.6	57.7

Fatherhood, as Blankenhorn points out, is the social role that obligates men to their biological offspring. Its demands, more than anything else, help men become good men, be good citizens, act altruistically rather than selfishly, and fulfill their destinies as sons of God. Unless maleness is tempered by responsible fatherhood, the result is narcissism, violence, predatory sexual behavior, and the rule of the strong over the weak. Furthermore, fatherhood, by supplementing and adding to the maternal investment in children, is essential for the normal development of offspring. Fathers physically protect their children and provide them with the food, clothing, shelter, and other material resources they cannot provide for themselves. It is a father's personal involvement in the lives of his children that gives them what only a father can contribute to their identity, character, and moral foundations. Further, on a day-to-day basis, fathers provide the essential nurturing and bonding associated with feeding, playing, story-telling, loving, and even diaper changing! Indeed, Margaret Mead insists that "every known human society rests firmly on the learned nurturing behaviour of men."[6]

The effects of fatherlessness are profound, both for men and for their offspring. The impacts on the young are especially distressing. They include the following:

Adolescent Childbearing

Adolescent childbearing is linked closely to the decline of fatherhood, not only because more males (both adolescent and adult) are willing to impregnate girls without the slightest intention of becoming an effective father but also because more girls are growing up without a father in the home. It is well-established that girls who grow up without fathers are at much greater risk for early sexual activity, adolescent childbearing, and divorce.[7] These findings are independent of economics: it is not lack of money but lack of a father that counts.

Domestic Violence against Women

The sickening and cowardly spectacle of men beating women is tragically common. We wince as we read of it nearly every day in our newspapers or watch reports of it on television. According to the Centers for Disease Control and Prevention, in 1994 about six percent of all pregnant women in the U.S. were battered by their "husbands or partners."[8] For every *married* pregnant woman who reported she was abused by her husband, almost four *unmarried* pregnant women reported being abused by their boyfriend. In other words, violent behavior by men toward women is strongly linked to marital status: married men are much less likely to beat the women in their lives than are unmarried men.

Childhood Poverty

A multitude of statistics and studies confirm that children in single-mother homes are much more likely to live in poverty than those in families with both parents present. In 1992, for example, about eight percent of the children of married couples in the United States lived in poverty; but in homes headed by a single mother about forty-six percent of the children lived in poverty.[9] The poverty experienced by single mothers is likely to be long-lasting. Single mothers remain single on average for roughly six years. In fact, only one-third of African American mothers remarry within ten years of separation. Furthermore, of never-married mothers who receive welfare benefits, about forty percent remain on the welfare rolls for ten years or more.* This welfare dependency tends to be passed on from one generation to another, from mother to daughter and granddaughter.

Most observers agree that the link between family structure and child poverty is one of cause and effect, not simply a statistical correlation. Simply put, fatherlessness, with all its attendant ramifications, causes child poverty. The best antipoverty program ever devised for children is to have a stable, intact family, with both father and mother present.

It is clear from the foregoing that the declining status and importance of fatherhood in our society does not bode well for the future. No society can long survive that denigrates, demeans, and devalues fatherhood. Men who do not look upon fatherhood, preceded by an honorable marriage, as a sacred privilege and obligation, deny their own manliness and can never rise to their divine potential, either in this world or the next.

Counsel on how to deal effectively with the grave problems affecting fathers is given in Part Two of this book (chapters 6–8).

* This statistic will of course change in light of recent (1996) changes in the length of time people are eligible for government welfare assistance.

3

MODERN GADIANTON ROBBERS:
CRIMINAL STREET GANGS
IN AMERICA

Secret combinations of groups of conspirators who plot and carry out "works of darkness" have been known since the days of Cain (see Moses 5:51). Indeed, as Moroni wrote, "it hath been made known to me that they [i.e. secret combinations] are had among *all people*" (Ether 8:20; emphasis added). The purpose of such conspiracies is and ever will be to get power and gain. Their author is Satan, "who stirreth up the children of men unto secret combinations of murder and all manner of secret works of darkness" (2 Nephi 9:9). The tools they employ include subversion of public virtue and legally constituted authority, fraud, murder, robbery, extortion, assault—every item in the long, lamentable catalogue of greed, crime, and corruption.

Perhaps the most well-known secret combination mentioned in the Book of Mormon is that of Gadianton, himself an expert in wickedness, who became the leader of a band of villains originally led by Kishkumen. So great was their power and evil influence, the Gadianton gang did "prove the overthrow, yea, almost the entire destruction of the people of Nephi" (Helaman 2:13).

Although the concerted efforts of the people succeeded in subduing for a time "Gadianton's robbers and murderers," as they came to be called (Helaman 6:18), in the last bloody

19

days of Nephite history they arose and spread again over the land (see 4 Nephi 1:42). Their devilish deeds contributed in a major way to the final destruction of the Nephites.

In our day, secret combinations are expressed most notably in organized criminal syndicates, such as the mafia, and in certain political and commercial organizations. Though such organizations have, as noted, plagued mankind since time immemorial, a more recent phenomenon is the rise of so-called youth[1] gangs. These groups display characteristics and patterns of behavior strikingly similar to those of the Gadianton robbers.

Criminal street gangs represent a new culture. For many "gangsters," the lifestyle they have adopted becomes a thrill-seeking, risk-taking way to express contempt for the status quo and to deliberately affront and insult those in society's mainstream. Although some rebellion against the structures and strictures of society is experienced by many youth as part of the process of growing up and expressing independence, gang members are characterized by their violent and destructive behavior. In the Salt Lake City area, for example, during 1995 there were 8,496 gang-related crimes, of which 2,130 were nongraffiti crimes.

Gang members are outlaws from mainstream society. The personal value system embraced by these young criminals values above all else loyalty and respect. The gang becomes, in effect, their family. Devotion to their "family" is expressed in unwavering, unquestionable loyalty to their "home boys" or "homies."

Closely related to loyalty is the issue of respect. The degree of self-worth and self-esteem held by gang members is determined by the degree to which they are able to command or demand respect. Gang members often are unable to differentiate between power and respect and believe that only if they obtain power over another person, often through fear and intimidation, will they be respected. Failure to acknowledge demands for respect prompts the expression of outlaw behavior. The gang member feels obligated to challenge, threaten, and perhaps commit violence against whoever dares to "diss" (disrespect) him/her.

Another noteworthy tenet of the gang culture is the belief held by many in an unalterable destiny, a road one is fated to go down until a point of incarceration or death is reached. Gangsters speak of "*mi locos vatos*" (my crazy life). This belief fuels the need to "eat, drink, and be merry, for tomorrow we die." It encourages getting what you want *now*, even at the expense of those who get in your way. This sense of fatalism also discourages long-term goals such as getting an education and making other provisions for the future. This attitude is reflected in the "smile now—cry later" tattoo frequently displayed by gang members.

Graffiti—the spray painting of slogans and names by gang members on public surfaces including buildings, fences, walls, desks, park benches, etc.—is of two basic types. The first, "gang" graffiti, is directly involved with gang culture and is generally confined to the specific neighborhood or "turf" of a dominant gang. It is used to "stake out" an area or neighborhood, to display ownership, to mark territory, and to show disrespect for other gangs or the police. In gang culture an act of perceived disrespect is a challenge to one's honor and requires a response by the offended party, almost always violent in nature. Gang graffiti is often called "the newspaper of the street" because it provides information on what is going on within local gang communities. It identifies gang members, their territory or "turf," alliances with other gangs, current enemies, attitudes toward the police, etc.

The second type of graffiti, "tagger" graffiti, is not confined

21

to a specific geographic area. "Taggers" strive for notoriety and name recognition. They adopt a specific nickname or moniker, which they use in signing or identifying their work. The harder or more dangerous the task, the more prestige is attached to the "tagger" and his associates (his "crew" or "posse").

Obviously, the lines between "gang" graffiti and "tagger" graffiti become blurred as the motivations of taggers and street gangsters—for recognition, excitement, notoriety, etc.— merge and become identical.

Graffiti is without doubt the most conspicuous gang-related crime—one that adversely affects community pride and introduces a sense of fear and insecurity. In order to bring control over the life of a community back into the hands of responsible, law-abiding citizens, it is essential that graffiti promptly be removed. In addition, every effort must be made to reduce the attractiveness of a neighborhood to the sprayers of graffiti. This can be done by the use of climbing shrubs (preferably with thorns) to cover walls; neighborhood watch programs; and the installation of outside lights, perhaps linked to lawn sprinkling systems; and so forth. To effectively combat graffiti, the community must take steps to minimize its visibility. When it is quickly removed, it makes the risk and effort involved in defacing public property discouraging to the perpetrators.

Street gang culture crosses all social boundaries. Although many gang members come from dysfunctional and/or minority families, often with low incomes, some come from apparently strong, traditional middle- or upper-class families. Furthermore, although the dominant percentage of gang members may come from minority racial or ethnic groups, the culture of criminal street gangs encompasses every hue of the ethnic rainbow. There are no racial, ethnic, cultural, age, gender, religious, socioeconomic, or geographic boundaries to gang membership.

The reasons why youth join gangs are complex. An important clue to the etiology of gangs lies in the fact that ethnic gangs developed in America following the arrival of each of the waves of foreign immigrants during the last hundred years or more. In general, most immigrants who achieved "the American dream" did so by legitimate means and moved within a generation or so into the mainstream of American life. But some of those who felt excluded from the larger society by reason of discrimination, poverty, language problems, etc., sought to escape their plight by illegitimate, criminal means.

The feelings of belonging to an ethnic underclass, excluded from the mainstream of American life, of being considered of little worth as a person, powerless, and disenfranchised, open the door to violence and other antisocial behavior. Under such conditions, joining a gang may give a sense of belonging, of power, of solidarity with others, and of family.

Those who become fully committed to the criminal street gang culture are, for practical purposes, beyond the reach of families, schools, churches, and social agencies, unless and until they want *with all their hearts* to change and become willing to persevere in a prolonged, conscious effort to do so. Those who wish to get out of a gang may face the threat of physical violence at the hands of other gang members. In some instances, they may be required to move away from their neighborhood and start life anew elsewhere.

Street gangs are typically involved in a broad variety of criminal activities, including drug trafficking, armed robberies, rape, intimidation, extortion, homicide, etc. They are in today's world increasingly well-armed; some gangs in the

23

United States have access to highly sophisticated weapons such as grenades, machine guns, rocket launchers, etc. The potential for effective terrorist activities by well-organized gangs is obvious.

Gang members often display tattoos and wear clothing associated with their particular organization. They may "flash" distinctive hand signals that instantly identify them both to friend and foe. It is wrong, however, to believe that all youth wearing baggy clothing—oversized pants that are worn low on the hips and the like—or who sport colored (usually red or blue) hats, bandanas, or other articles of clothing, are necessarily involved in a gang; although they *may* be. Such clothing is popular among today's youth, both with those who belong to gangs and those who do not. However, naive youngsters, who are not "gangsters" but wear clothing associated with the gang culture, may give the false impression to real gang members that they are affiliated with a gang. This may put the individual involved at considerable personal risk.

The impact of gang activities on other law-abiding youth can turn the lives of the victims into nightmares. Extortion, threats, bullying, and assaults are common. The following two incidents, taken from the proceedings of the 1993 Gang Conference of the Salt Lake Area Gang Project, illustrate what is all too common.

At a Salt Lake City elementary school, a fifth grader refused to go to school because a classmate threatened that his older brother's gang would kill him. The victim's error: he had accidentally bumped into the other student on the playground!

In another incident, also in the Salt Lake City area, a seventh-grade girl refused to join a neighborhood gang and became the target of extortion. The gang also threatened to kill her and her family if she divulged to anyone their tactics of terror and intimidation. Not surprisingly, the girl began to fall apart psychologically under the strain. Her school grades plummeted, and she became progressively more withdrawn in class. Finally, her teacher was able to learn of the torment and put an end to it.

The fear felt by children who live in gang-infested neighborhoods is told with the honesty and openness of childhood in the following true story:

> In my neighborhood there is a lot of shooting and three people got shot. On the next day when I was going to school I saw a little stream of blood on the ground. One day after school me and my mother had to dodge bullets. I was not scared.
>
> There is a church and a school that I go to in my neighborhood. There are robbers that live in my building, they broke into our house twice. There are rowhouses in my neighborhood and a man got shot, and he was dead. On another day I saw a boy named Zak get shot. By King High School Susan Harris got shot and she died. It was in the newspaper. When me and my mother was going to church we could see the fire from the guns being shot in 4414 building. I was not scared. In my neighborhood there are too many fights. I have never been in a fight before. There are many trees in my neighborhood.
>
> God is going to come back one day and judge the world. Not just my neighborhood.
>
> I know these are really, really bad things, but I have some good things in my neighborhood. Like sometimes my neighborhood is peaceful and quiet and there is no shooting. When me and my mother and some friends go to the lake we have a lot of fun. Sometimes the children in my building go to Sunday School with me and my mother. Also the building I live in is so tall I can see downtown and the lake. It looks so pretty.

I believe in God and I know one day we will be in a gooder place than we are now.[2]

Finally, a word about girls and gangs. Females may be full-fledged members of gangs or be associated with them. They are used not only as sex objects by male gangsters but increasingly as couriers, who carry weapons and drugs on their persons for male gang members, in the belief they are less likely to be searched by male law enforcement officers. They may also be used to lure or entice rival gangsters into an ambush.

There are, however, all-girl gangs. One that comes to mind is the infamous Krazy Rose Park Queens, a Salt Lake area female gang. I talked to two members of that group recently while visiting the juvenile prison at Decker Lake, Utah, where I attended a Sunday School class with them. Both were in prison for armed robbery. Their copies of the scriptures were well-read, and the girls were obviously familiar with them. These two young women, both soft-spoken and polite, unwittingly demonstrated the ability of gang members to compartmentalize their lives. They saw no dissonance, no incongruity, between their membership in a gang and their deep commitment to the Church. Church was for Sundays, and the rest of the week was for the gang.

Against the background of this necessarily brief and sketchy outline of gang culture, let us now examine how gang behavior parallels that of the Gadianton robbers who did so much damage to Nephite society. Sociological information is of great value in helping us understand how gangs function and what motivates gang members. But it is well to keep in mind that behind it all stands the menacing, malignant figure of the adversary, the "founder of murder and works of darkness." Gangs are literally the devil's work. That is not to say, of course, that all gang members are the conscious, direct agents of the devil. Far from it. But we can be sure that, figuratively speaking at least, he rubs his hands in glee at their deeds of darkness. The scriptures cited below make clear the association between the deeds and behavior of the Gadianton robbers and those of contemporary gang members:

Loyalty to Fellow Gang Members

"Satan did stir up the hearts of the more part of the Nephites, insomuch that they did unite with those bands of robbers, and did enter into their covenants and their oaths, that they would protect and preserve one another in whatsoever difficult circumstances they should be placed, that they should not suffer for their murders, and their plunderings, and their stealings" (Helaman 6:21).

An Outlaw Society with Its Own Laws

"And whosoever of those who belonged to their band should reveal unto the world of their wickedness and their abominations, should be tried, not according to the laws of their country, but according to the laws of their wickedness, . . . And it came to pass that all these iniquities did come unto them in the space of not many years" (Helaman 6:24, 32).

Signs and Signals

"They did have their signs, yea, their secret signs, and their secret words; and this that they might distinguish a brother who had entered into the covenant, that whatsoever wickedness his brother should do he should not be injured by his brother, nor by those who did belong to his band, who had taken this covenant. And thus they might murder, and plunder, and steal, and commit whoredoms and all manner

27

of wickedness, contrary to the laws of their country and also the laws of their God" (Helaman 6:22–23).

Distinctive Clothing

"And they were girded about after the manner of robbers; and they had a lamb-skin about their loins, and they were dyed in blood, and their heads were shorn, and they had headplates upon them" (3 Nephi 4:7).

Recruitment Activities

"And there was also a cause of much sorrow among the Lamanites; for behold, they had many children who did grow up and began to wax strong in years, that they became for themselves, and were led away by some who were Zoramites, by their lyings and their flattering words, to join those Gadianton robbers" (3 Nephi 1:29).

A Spreading Menace

"And these Gadianton robbers, who were among the Lamanites, did infest the land, insomuch that the inhabitants thereof began to hide up their treasures in the earth" (Mormon 1:18).

Can anyone doubt that the criminal street gangs that "infest the land" represent the modern counterpart of the Gadianton robbers of old?

The Special Burdens Borne by Children

Although all of society suffers from the activities of criminal gangs, children suffer perhaps most, both as victims of gang violence and as tragic participants lured into gang activity. Law enforcement officers indicate that gang members often will entice younger children into carrying out the most dangerous activities such as being the shooter in drive-by shootings, in the belief they will receive lighter treatment if apprehended.

Children deserve and have a right to peace and security. The great prophet Isaiah intoned, "And all thy children shall be taught of the LORD; and great shall be the peace of thy children" (Isaiah 54:13).

And Jesus himself declared, "Even so it is not the will of your Father which is in heaven, that one of these little ones should perish" (Matthew 18:14).

Jesus' great love for children is illustrated with great poignancy by this tender passage from the Book of Mormon:

"And it came to pass that he commanded that their little children should be brought. So they brought their little children and set them down upon the ground round about him, and Jesus stood in the midst . . . and he took their little children, one by one, and blessed them, and prayed unto the Father for them. And when he had done this he wept again; And he spake unto the multitude, and said unto them: Behold your little ones . . . and they saw angels descending out of heaven as it were in the midst of fire; and they came down and encircled those little ones about, and they were encircled about with fire; and the angels did minister unto them" (3 Nephi 17:11-12, 21-24).

Modern-day prophets have lifted their voices in pleading on behalf of children. President Gordon B. Hinckley said:

"My plea—and I wish I were more eloquent in voicing it—is a plea to save the children. Too many of them walk with pain and fear, in loneliness and despair. Children need sunlight. They need happiness. They need love and nurture. They need kindness and refreshment and affection. Every home, regardless of the cost of the house, can provide an environment of love which will be an environment of salvation" (*Ensign,* November 1994, 54).

Is there anything we can do to combat the modern Gadianton robbers who comprise today's criminal street gangs? We should not despair, much can be done. Chapter 7 provides some counsel.

4

THE DECLINING ROLE OF RELIGION IN SOCIETY

President James E. Faust has noted that in contrast to earlier, God-fearing times, a new civil religion seems to be developing in America. He said: "The civil religion I refer to is a secular religion. It has no moral absolutes. It is nondenominational. It is non-theistic. It is politically focused. It is antagonistic to religion. It rejects the historic religious traditions of America. It feels strange. If this trend continues, nonbelief will be more honored than belief. While all beliefs must be protected, are atheism, agnosticism, cynicism, and moral relativism to be more safeguarded and valued than Christianity, Judaism, and the tenets of Islam, which hold that there is a Supreme Being and that mortals are accountable to him? If so, this would, in my opinion, place America in great moral jeopardy."[1]

The secularism that is so aggressively being promoted rejects the historical religious traditions of the nation, is openly antagonistic toward religion based upon belief in God and his commandments, and has a definite political axe to grind. This "secular religion" seeks to trivialize and marginalize belief in God and ridicules religious people as either credulous fools or conniving knaves.

Such secularism is a relatively new phenomenon in America. Until recently, prevailing public attitudes toward

31

religion in America were generally respectful. A case in point: I enjoyed recently watching again a movie entitled *Heaven Knows, Mr. Allison*, produced in 1957 and starring Robert Mitchum and Deborah Kerr. The movie depicts the adventures of a U.S. Marine (Mitchum) and a Catholic nun (Kerr) stranded on a Japanese-occupied island somewhere in the Pacific during World War II. Though the man and the woman are attracted to each other, there is no hanky-panky, no impropriety, none of the sexual promiscuity and casual coarseness seen in many movies produced today. Mitchum is a perfect gentleman, bound by his loyalty to the Corps; Kerr a perfect lady, bound by her loyalty to her religious vocation. Kerr's religious beliefs, though portrayed as largely incomprehensible to Mitchum, are referred to in terms of the respect that they deserve. Both the marine and the nun display a nobility of character and an integrity, which leaves viewers of the film exalted rather than in need of a good wash. How things have changed, for the worse, in the last forty years!

The Status of Religion in Modern America

What then is the status of religion in modern American society? Is it healthy or in need of rejuvenation and renewal? For more than fifty years the Princeton Religion Research Center and the Gallup Poll have studied religious behavior and opinion in America. Each year up to 40,000 interviews are held with representative nationwide samples of men and women, ages eighteen and older. From eight fundamental measurements of religious behavior, a composite average index is calculated as a means of tracking broad trends over time. Some of the indicators examined have been found to be remarkably constant from year to year, while others have changed markedly in reaction to events, both secular and

32

religious. In 1991 the index stood at 656 out of a theoretically possible 1,000, up modestly (by 5 to 6 points) over the previous three years, when it had reached an all-time low.

The current status of the individual components that go to make up the index may be summarized as follows:

- Belief in God, however defined, is unusually high in America, ranging from 94–99% of adults over the last fifty years.

- Approximately nine in ten adults say there is a religious denomination or faith they prefer. This level has stayed relatively constant since 1947.

- Only six of ten adults feel that religion is able to answer today's problems. This indicator of religious faith has ranged widely over time, from as high as 81% in 1957 to a low of 56% in 1984.

- Approximately 2/3 of the adult population claim to now be members of a church, synagogue, or similar place of worship.

- In 1993 about 55% of adults had confidence in a church or "organized religion." Confidence in churches was severely tested during the 1980s, as scandals involving certain televangelists and doctrinal or policy differences within denominations were widely reported in the media.

- Confidence in the clergy also suffered during the 1980s but has risen somewhat in more recent years. In 1993 just over half of those surveyed expressed confidence in the integrity and honesty of the clergy.

- Although three Americans in four questioned in the early 1950s said that religion was very important in their lives, that figure stood in 1993 at just under 60%.

- Approximately 40% of the adult population attended a place of worship during a typical week in 1993.

Denominational switching is common in the United States. The Princeton Religion Research Center has noted that about one adult in four has changed faiths or denominations at least once from the religion in which he or she was raised. For the most part these switches have benefitted Protestant denominations, with nine times as many becoming Protestants as become Catholics.

Roof and McKinney have examined in detail current religious trends in America.[2] They note that religious individualism is characteristic of contemporary life in this country. Involvement within a religious institution seems of decreasing significance. Another author puts it this way: "The mainline denominations are bleeding. Their churches have more pew than flock, and unless they change, they have more history than future. Little congregations of fewer than a hundred at worship in rural communities and inner cities are shutting their doors at the rate of fifty a week, by one estimate."[3]

Religion in America is becoming increasingly a matter of personal choice and conscience, with people "shopping around," picking a little here and a little there from one denomination or another, discarding what they don't like and keeping what appeals to them. Thus, many American Catholics, who still consider themselves to be "good Catholics," reject the teachings of their church on such matters as abortion and divorce, viewing such issues to be private matters outside of the purview and authority of their church.

The long-standing synthesis of religion and culture that has existed since almost the beginning of the nation is crumbling. Ascriptive factors, such as race, ethnicity, social class, and region, which have long been of major importance in determining religious affiliation in America, are becoming less important. Perhaps in part this change relates to the general weakening of traditional social roots and ties in this country. What the end result of these changes will be is still difficult to ascertain, but one thing is certain: the consequences for many churches are and will be important.

Considerable evidence indicates that people with strong religious convictions are more resistant to physical and social ills than are nonbelievers. The well-known reduced incidence of heart disease and most cancers among practicing American Latter-day Saints is a case in point. A recent editorial in *The Wall Street Journal*, 6 March 1996, entitled "Drugs and God," pointed out that drug abuse is not just a social problem but rather is a moral problem requiring a moral solution. The writer notes that in the inner city, churches are often the only institutions that still work, albeit imperfectly, and adds, "Religion gives people, particularly teenagers, what they most need to combat drugs, a reason to say no."

Before leaving this brief discussion of the current status of religion in America, it is important to note that Americans express considerable unease about the ethics and moral standards of the populace. In 1,000 interviews conducted by the Princeton Group in 1991, only thirty-three percent of respondents expressed satisfaction with the ethical and moral standards of the American people; only twenty-four percent were satisfied with the honesty and standards of behavior in this country; and only thirteen percent were satisfied with our care of the poor and needy.

The Spiritual Malaise in American Society

From the foregoing it seems fair to state that while religious *practice* in America is flourishing, religious *behavior*—behavior that comes from deep and abiding religious faith—is much more narrowly based. It is important to consider the reasons for this discrepancy.

Many thoughtful observers have noted the increased coarseness, vulgarity, gratuitous violence, pessimism, and cynicism evident in our society. A growing percentage of Americans have lost confidence in the capacity of government, industry, and churches to provide solutions. A recent story in the *Deseret News,* March 8, 1996, illustrates the point. An organization calling itself "Campaign for America" has been asking groups of citizens about their views on the future. When asked what makes her most angry, one woman in a recently convened "focus group" replied without hesitation, "The sadness of America." Few thought their children would do better. One man said, "I feel that I probably lived in the golden age of America, and that young people are probably not going to see that." "Downhill," one after another said when asked how things are going for the nation.

There *is* a pessimistic and anxious mood abroad in the country. The *ethos* of America—its moral, spiritual and aesthetic character and habits—is ill and in serious need of treatment.

There are, perhaps, nearly as many diagnosticians of what is wrong with our society as there are chroniclers of the unraveling of the moral fabric of America. Materialism, drugs, permissiveness, Marx, Freud, a lack of credible role models, the transiency of our society, self-indulgence, technological change, which leaves many feeling alienated and adrift, humanism—you name it; all have been indicted.

I submit that the real reason for the crisis of our time is spiritual malaise—a spiritual anomie, an exhaustion of the soul. People experience but do not learn. This spiritual apathy is described by the word *acedia. Acedia* comes from the Greek, *a* (not) plus *kédos* (care)—hence, not caring, boredom, or apathy. In its modern usage *acedia* refers to sloth, one of the Seven Deadly Sins enumerated by Thomas Aquinas in his *Summa Theologiae.*

More instructively for our purposes, *acedia* also means spiritual torpor. But *acedia* signifies more than just spiritual laziness or even indifference. It connotes misplaced priorities, a darkening of the soul, a hatred of the good, a rejection of spiritual things, which leads ultimately to a cankering of the soul, bringing sadness, ill temper, and death of the heart. It is termed a "deadly sin" by some because it is "an oppressive sorrow that so weighs upon a man's mind that he wants not to exercise any virtue." It leads to spiritual paralysis.[4] It is related to that condition described by Nephi when he said that Laman and Lemuel "were past feeling" (1 Nephi 17:45).

Acedia, a sour, ill-tempered rejection of spiritual things, manifests itself in the querulous assertion that only secular arguments should be entertained on moral questions. It is seen in the mean-spirited shouting down in a public forum of those who use arguments based on religious beliefs to object to homosexual or other immoral activities. Yet, as Richard John Neuhaus has pointed out: "In a democracy that is free and robust, an opinion is no more disqualified for being 'religious' than for being atheistic, or psychoanalytic, or Marxist, or just plain dumb. There is no legal or constitutional question about the admission of religion to the public square; there is only a question about the free and equal participation of citizens in our public business."[5] In my view *acedia* lies behind Aleksandr Solzhenitsyn's concerns about what he terms a "relentless cult of novelty" in art, with its assertion that art need not be good or pure, just so long as it is new, newer, and newer still. Such art, Solzhenitsyn asserts, "conceals an unyielding and long-sustained attempt to undermine, ridicule and uproot all moral precepts. There is no God, there is no truth, the universe is chaotic, all is relative.

37

. . . How clamorous it all is, but also—how helpless."[6] Widespread feelings of *acedia* lead inevitably both to cynicism and to reduced capacity for shock, disgust, and outrage—an anesthesia of the soul that inures one to the sufferings of others. During the riots in Los Angeles in 1992, for example, two men were filmed pulling a truck driver from his truck, crushing his skull with a brick, and then doing a victory dance over his unconscious body. They were successfully defended in the courts on the basis that people cannot be held accountable for getting caught up in mob violence. They were just in the wrong place at the wrong time—themselves victims more than criminals, it was claimed successfully.

What is happening in our society, then, is "a corruption of the heart, a turning away in the soul. Our aspirations, our affections, and our desires are turned toward the wrong things."[7]

Abraham Lincoln, one of the noblest sons this nation or any other has ever produced, understood, as de Tocqueville had observed more than a century before Lincoln's presidency, that America will be great only to the extent that it is good. In designating and setting apart a day for National Prayer and Humiliation in 1863, Lincoln declared in words that apply equally to our time: "We have grown in number, wealth, and power as no other Nation has ever grown. But we have forgotten God. We have forgotten the gracious hand which preserved us in peace and multiplied and enriched and strengthened us, and we have vainly imagined, in the deceitfulness of our hearts, that all these blessings were produced by some superior wisdom and virtue of our own. Intoxicated with unbroken success we have become too self-sufficient to feel the necessity of redeeming and preserving grace, too proud to pray to the God that made us!"[8]

Perhaps *acedia*—spiritual torpor and apathy—can be

explained in part by the failure of some who profess religious belief to be *spiritually* in tune. Under such circumstances, though those involved may draw near to God with their lips, their hearts are frequently far from Him. "They teach for doctrines the commandments of men, having a form of godliness, but they deny the power thereof" (JS–H 1:19). Like the seed that fell upon stony places in the parable of the sower (Matthew 13:4–8), they have "no deepness of earth: and when the sun was up, they were scorched; and because they had no root, they withered away." Those so involved may have given mental assent, but they have not experienced the "mighty change of heart" needed for true spiritual commitment. Only with that commitment can the storms of adversity found in every life successfully be weathered and the growing disdain for spiritual things, which characterizes our society, be overcome.

5

THE END RESULT: DECLINE AND DECAY

There can be little doubt that there has been a palpable and frightening decline in the moral and spiritual health of American society over the last thirty years. Self-control has given way to self-indulgence. The institutions in society that traditionally have had the greatest influence on the public's beliefs, attitudes, and behavior—home, school, community, and church—have quite simply become enfeebled and in many instances impotent. Quoting pollster Daniel Yakelovitch, William J. Bennett sums up what has happened by stating, "Our society now places less value than before on what we owe to others as a matter of moral obligation; less value on sacrifice as a moral good; less value on social conformity, respectability, and observing the rules; and less value on correctness and restraint in matters of physical pleasure and sexuality."[1]

We live in a time when we are in the midst of a so-called "sexual revolution," and ours has become a society saturated with sex. Perhaps the key presupposition upon which this "revolution" rests is the fallacy that sexual desire must be acted upon and satisfied promptly. Any suggestion that discipline, denial, or restraint are essential is popularly depicted as unhealthy and repressive. Long-established standards of sexual behavior and decency, both inside and outside of marriage, are ignored and dishonored with little or no societal reproach being brought against those who act outrageously or irresponsibly. In our day, the place of sex in life is grotesquely exaggerated and at the same time trivialized. That sacred function has to our detriment been reduced by many to a matter of recreation or made into a pastime—something that exists for pleasure alone. Such an attitude, one that defines men and women only in terms of sexual desires, demeans and dehumanizes both sexes and denies the divinity that is within all of God's children. Unbridled sexual indulgence also diminishes the importance and sanctity of marriage and erodes the order and discipline marriage has always imposed on society. In fact, indulging in casual sex flies in the face of all that civilization has learned about preserving and benefiting the human race.

The major sea change that has occurred in American society during the past three decades portends even more drastic and harmful events in the future. This is a time when "darkness covereth the earth, and gross darkness the minds of the people, and all flesh has become corrupt before my face" (D&C 112:23). Our society, drenched with sin and wickedness, is proceeding apace down the long stairway which, in Winston Churchill's words given in another context, "leads to a dark gulf. It is a fine, broad stairway at the beginning, but after a bit the carpet wears. A little further there are only flagstones and a little further on still, they break beneath your feet."[2]

Alexander Pope gave poetic expression to the sort of attitudinal and behavioral changes now taking place in America when he wrote these familiar lines:

> Vice is a monster of so frightful mien,
> As to be hated needs but to be seen;

Yet seen too oft, familiar with her face,
We first endure, then pity, then embrace.

I have asserted that the institutions in society that traditionally have had the greatest influence on the public's beliefs, attitudes, and priorities, including churches, have become enfeebled and in many instances impotent to reverse the changes sweeping the nation. The Ramsey Colloquium, a group of noted Jewish and Christian theologians, philosophers, and scholars, has commented on the complicity of religious communities and leadership in the United States in the demeaning of the social norms essential for a healthy society, decrying "religious communities that have in recent decades winked at promiscuity (even among the clergy), that have solemnly repeated marriage vows that their own congregations do not take seriously, and that have failed to concern themselves with the devastating effects of divorce upon children." The Colloquium calls for a "renewal of integrity, in teaching and practice, regarding traditional sexual ethics."[3]

Signs of the Times

We witness daily the unleashing of the "natural man," with his carnality and sensuality. These, the "last days," are the time of the adversary's power, a time of surging self-indulgence and selfishness on a perhaps unprecedented scale. Selfishness, Elder Neal A. Maxwell, has pointed out, "activates all the cardinal sins. It is the detonator in the breaking of the Ten Commandments."[4]

In his second letter to Timothy, Paul spoke of the last days—the perilous times in which we live: "For men shall be lovers of their own selves, covetous, boasters, proud, blasphemers, disobedient to parents, unthankful, unholy, without natural affection, trucebreakers, false accusers, incontinent, fierce, despisers of those that are good, traitors, heady, highminded, lovers of pleasures more than lovers of God; having a form of godliness; but denying the power thereof: from such turn away" (2 Timothy 3:2–5).

Consider how selfishness facilitates and augments each of the sins enumerated above. He who is selfish has an inordinate love for himself; is covetous, boastful, conceited, unthankful, and filled with contempt for others. These all come easily to him as do the other faults mentioned by Paul. Selfishness brings other problems as well, one of which is untreatable, self-serving stubbornness, best described as pigheadedness, a fault that "is as iniquity and idolatry," as the prophet Samuel reminded Saul (see 1 Samuel 15:23). Indeed, one who exhibits that degree of stubbornness worships himself and not God.

Selfishness and pride go together as unholy handmaidens of the adversary. Both have at their core enmity toward God and our fellowman. "The proud," President Ezra Taft Benson noted, "make every man their adversary by pitting their intellects, opinions, works, wealth, talents, or any other worldly measuring device against others."[5] Those words apply with equal power to the selfish.

We Are Not Immune

The Latter-day Saints, it is sad to say, are not immune to the temptations of the world. Speaking over a century ago, President John Taylor warned us of the need to turn away from the world and to follow the ways of the Lord. He said: "We are not here to follow the devices and desires of our own hearts; we are not here to carry out any particular theory of our own; we are not here to build up any system of man's creation; but we are here simply to do the will of God in the establishment of his kingdom on the earth. In many things however we have not lived up to that high and glorious privilege which has been presented to us; we have been careless and indifferent, and it seems as though Satan has been permitted to try and tempt us in every possible way. For a few years past a spirit of greed and covetousness has run through the land and cursed as with a withering blight every thing it has touched. It is as bad in its effects upon the mind of man as any pestilence or plague upon the human body. We have begun to run after the things of the world; our hearts, feelings and affections, in many instances, have been estranged from God. It is time that something should transpire to wake us up to a sense of the position we occupy; it is time we realized how God and angels look upon men who are absorbed in the things of this world instead of living up to their professions and the covenants they have made with him."[6]

President Taylor's words echo the warnings Elder Orson Pratt delivered in 1855: "There are individuals in this Territory, of a careless disposition, and you may mark them, and those that have waxed fat, and their hearts are upon the things of this world, that when tribulations come, they will be the ones to quake and fear, while those who have taken a different course will be able to stand.

"I heard brother Joseph, when speaking of those that were sick in Nauvoo, make remarks similar to those that I have now made. He said, that those who would not, when in good health, call upon the Lord, and acknowledge His hand in all things, and remember him, would not have faith when it was needed—he said that those individuals would have but very little faith in the days of their calamities and affliction.

"How often I have thought of the remark made by the Prophet; nothing can be more true than that remark; it carries its own evidence with it, that those individuals who have wealth and riches in abundance, but do not remember the

Lord, when troubles come, they will be in the greatest distress, generally speaking."[7]

What the prophets have foreseen has come to pass. In our schools, in the workplace, and in our neighborhoods, we are often surrounded by evil, those who deride or mock our most sacred beliefs, and public policy that is misguided and unlikely to achieve its stated aims because it is not based on true principles. It has ever been thus—opposition has always been part of the Christian struggle. Forewarned, we must meet the challenge and resist the forces that would erode our faith or draw us away from what we know to be true. In a period of brutal discouragement, Joseph Smith was comforted by the Lord with an assurance that his friends would yet stand by him, offering him their "warm hearts and friendly hands" (D&C 121:9). Thanks be to God for faithful friends and family members and for a divinely revealed pattern of worship that provides a way for us to "meet together often" to renew our friendships, draw strength from one another, and "partake of bread and [water] in the remembrance of the Lord Jesus" (D&C 20:75).

ROLLING BACK
THE DARKNESS

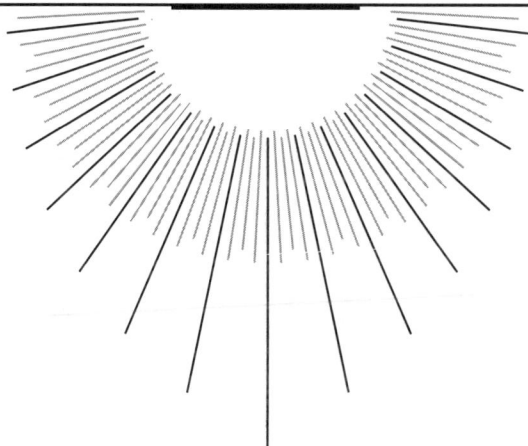

6

IT STARTS WITH ME

What can we do, as individuals, families, and the people of Christ, to push back the world, to combat the spreading evil that threatens to engulf us all? There are no ready answers, no magic buttons to press. The road ahead is long and hard, and we will surely suffer casualties along the way. However, a few principles may serve as guideposts on our journey.

Public and Private Morality
Have Their Foundations in Religion

No man or woman can maintain personal morality unless his or her actions flow out of a genuine religious faith and are based on eternal religious principles. Those who are not so based will eventually be tripped up by the moral relativism of situational ethics. This may sound like an extreme position, but it is one that the scriptures proclaim and history affirms. "Except the Lord build the house, they labour in vain that build it" (Psalm 127:1).

In his address of 19 September 1796, given as he prepared to leave office, President George Washington spoke about the importance of morality to the country's well-being, "Whatever may be conceded to the influence of refined education . . . reason and experience both forbid us to expect that National morality can prevail in exclusion of religious principle." Washington also said: "Of all the dispositions and habits which lead to political prosperity, Religion and Morality are indispensable supports. . . . And let us with caution indulge the supposition that morality can be maintained without religion. . . . Can it be, that Providence has not connected the permanent felicity of a Nation with its virtue?"[1]

According to James Madison, often referred to as the father of the American Constitution: "We have staked the whole future of American civilization, not upon the power of government, far from it. We have staked the future [of all of our political institutions] upon the capacity of each and all of us to govern ourselves, to sustain ourselves, according to the Ten Commandments of God."[2]

To the extent that this nation weakens or abandons the religious foundations on which it was based, it will surely fail and eventually fall. By contrast, any nation that keeps God's commandments and walks in his ways will prosper. Our whole Western system of laws and jurisprudence flows from our Judeo-Christian heritage as set forth in the Old and New Testaments. The strength of America is neither basically political nor legal. The foundation of this land, whether the citizenry wish to admit it or not, is spiritual. When that foundation is weakened, the future of the nation itself is put in jeopardy.

Most observers agree that the roots of Western society go back to ancient Greece and Rome. In a myriad of ways the contributions of those ancient states are permanently woven into the fabric of our modern society. Although we admittedly are the heirs of the Greco-Roman world, modern Western societies trace their direct spiritual and cultural ancestries to the contributions of Judeo-Christian thought as it developed from the teachings of the Hebrew prophets and Jesus of Nazareth.

In no country are Judeo-Christian contributions to every aspect of society of greater importance than in the United States of America. The early colonists, who came to America from Europe in the seventeenth century, journeyed here to fulfill their religious faith, to obtain the liberty to worship God according to the dictates of their consciences. For over two centuries, Americans have held fast to our founding fathers' belief in freedom for all people—a belief that springs directly from their spiritual heritage. John Adams, our second president, wrote in 1789, "Our Constitution was designed only for a moral and religious people. It is wholly inadequate for the government of any other."[3] The French jurist and historian, Alexis de Tocqueville, who traveled America in the early nineteenth century, stated, "Religion in America takes no direct part in the government of society, but it must be regarded as the first of their political institutions; for if it does not impart a taste for freedom, it facilitates the use of it."[4]

What, then, are the major contributions of Judeo-Christian thought to modern political and social principles and practices? Some of the most important contributions include the following concepts:

The Concept of the Fatherhood of God and the Brotherhood of Mankind

God, who created humankind in his own image, gave his sons and daughters their moral agency—the right to choose for themselves. His very nature forbids God from creating slaves. An ancient American prophet, Samuel the Lamanite, described mankind's freedom of choice as follows: "And now remember, remember, my brethren, that whosoever perisheth, perisheth unto himself; and whosoever doeth iniquity, doeth it unto himself; for behold, ye are free; ye are permitted to act for yourselves; for behold, God hath given unto you a knowledge and he hath made you free. He hath given unto you that ye might know good from evil, and he hath given unto you that ye might choose life or death; and ye can do good and be restored unto that which is good, or have that which is good restored unto you; or ye can do evil, and have that which is evil restored unto you" (Helaman 14:30–31).

The practical results of this belief in God, who created his sons and daughters "in his image," and endowed them with moral agency, include the following:

Liberty Is the Inherent Right of All of God's Children

Thomas Jefferson put it this way, "The God who gave us life gave us liberty." Any system of government that denies liberty denigrates man and denies God. Margaret Thatcher, former British Prime Minister, has observed that societies founded on the basis of morality and freedom prosper, but those that are not founded on those principles do not survive for long, as witness the recent demise of the Soviet Union, though they may do much harm during their existence.[5]

The Progression of Mankind

The concept of progress is neither Greek nor Roman; both viewed history as an endless cycle, without any notion of progress. The idea of historical progress is rooted in Jewish and Christian thought. As God's nature forbids him to create slaves, so too it forbids him creating sons and daughters intrinsically and eternally destined to be forever his inferiors. God's work and glory is to bring to pass the immortality and eternal life of his children, to have them share in his glory, growing ever more like him, progressing toward Godhood itself. Jesus said, "Be ye therefore perfect, even as your Father which is in Heaven is perfect" (Matthew 5:48), and to the Romans Paul wrote, "We are the children of God: and if children, then heirs; heirs of God, and joint-heirs with Christ" (Romans 8:16–17). The view that mankind's eternal destiny is to progress, that in a sense our very nature demands it, and further that history, as we know it on earth, has a beginning and an end, puts new perspective on who men and women are and what they may become and underlines the urgency on spending our mortal probation in endeavors that will further our eternal progression.

God Hath Made of One Blood All Nations of Men

In Judeo-Christian thought, God grants a fundamental equality to all human beings. With him there is no hierarchy of position, station, inheritance, or worldly honor. The American Declaration of Independence reflects this idea: "We hold these truths to be self-evident, that all men are created equal." The founding fathers did not, of course, suffer from the dangerous illusion that all men are equal in terms of talents and abilities. Common experience teaches otherwise: there is, after all, only one Michael Jordan! But the signers of the Declaration of Independence believed passionately that all of mankind possess inalienable rights, including life, liberty, and the pursuit of happiness; and that men and women are, by reason of those rights, considered equal before the law. The language of the Declaration of Independence, in spirit at least, has its origin in these words of the Apostle Paul to the Athenians: "God that made the world and all things therein . . . hath made of one blood all nations of men for to dwell on all the face of the earth, and hath determined the times before appointed, and the bounds of their habitation" (Acts 17:24, 26). The Prophet Nephi, unknown though he was by the signers of the Declaration of Independence, expressed much the same thought concerning the human race: "He [God] inviteth them all to come unto him and partake of his goodness; and he denieth none that come unto him, black and white, bond and free, male and female; and he remembereth the heathen; and all are alike unto God" (2 Nephi 26:33).

The Judeo-Christian concept of the equality yet uniqueness of every human soul differs from Communist notions of man, which pull all down to the same level and enforce uniformity.

The Concept of Compassion

In most religious traditions, concern for the suffering of others is limited to one's own family, clan, tribe, faith group, or nation. Christ's concept of compassion, however, puts no limit on it. In the noblest and most exalted expressions ever voiced of God's concern for all and of our mutual interdependence, Jesus said:

- "Love your enemies, bless them that curse you, do good to them that hate you, and pray for them which despitefully use you, and persecute you" (Matthew 5:44).
- Care for the hungry, the naked, the sick, the stranger, the prisoner (see Matthew 25:31–45).
- "By this shall all men know that ye are my disciples, if ye have love one to another" (John 13:35).
- "Greater love hath no man than this, that a man lay down his life for his friends" (John 15:13).
- To one who inquired, "Who is my neighbour?" Jesus recounted the story of the good Samaritan. After others—a priest and a Levite—had passed by a man who lay wounded, without helping, it was the

despised Samaritan who bound up his wounds, brought him to an inn, took care of him, and left funds for his further care. Then said Jesus, "Which now of these three, thinkest thou, was neighbour unto him that fell among the thieves?" The listener, his vision enlarged, replied, "He that shewed mercy on him." Then said Jesus unto him, "Go, and do thou likewise" (Luke 10:29–37).

- "If any man shall take of the abundance which I have made, and impart not his portion, according to the law of my gospel, unto the poor and the needy, he shall, with the wicked, lift up his eyes in hell, being in torment" (D&C 104:18).

The Concept of Absolute Truth

"I am the way, the truth, and the life," Jesus proclaimed (John 14:6), and Moses said, "Ascribe ye greatness unto our God. He is the Rock, his work is perfect: for all his ways are judgment: a God of truth and without iniquity, just and right is he" (Deuteronomy 32:3–4). President John Adams noted that in giving to the world the notion of God as the source of all truth, the Hebrews laid before the human race the possibilities of civilization. Truth is independent of temporal power, riches, or worldly position. It comes from God; he is its author. There *are* moral absolutes. Speaking to Brigham Young University students, Rex E. Lee, former university president, said this about absolute truth: "There are in this life some absolutes, things that never change, regardless of time, place, or circumstances. They are eternal truths, eternal principles—and, as Paul tells us, they are and will be the same yesterday, today, and forever."[6]

In his usual thoughtful, insightful way, Elder Dallin H. Oaks has reminded us: "One of the consequences of shifting

ROLLING BACK THE DARKNESS

from *moral absolutes* to *moral relativism* in public policy is that this produces a corresponding shift of emphasis from *responsibilities* to *rights*. Responsibilities originate in moral absolutes. In contrast, rights find their origin in legal principles, which are easily manipulated by moral relativism."[7]

The understanding that there are absolute truths empowers humankind; it frees them to search for truth, albeit truth as seen by mortal eyes as "through a glass, darkly (1 Corinthians 13:12). It encourages education as a search for truth, teaching us of our own finite limitations while assisting us in reaching for the ultimate truth, the Divine. "Now I know in part; but then shall I know even as also I am known" (*ibid.*).

A shared search for truth unites individuals of differing backgrounds and implies civilized social intercourse between those whose visions of truth may differ. It teaches humility, a decent respect for the opinions of others, a willingness to learn of truth "where'er 'tis found, whether on Christian or on heathen ground." It helps us love, or at least better understand, those, who like ourselves, seek for truth, each in his or her own way.

It is ironic that many in today's world no longer believe there is absolute truth. To today's cynics, all things, including right and wrong, are relative. Every assertion of right or wrong is open to debate.

The only absolutes for many today are power and self-interest. Studies done at the Princeton Religion Research Center show that about seven American adults in ten believe there are few moral absolutes and that matters of what is right or wrong must be judged as each situation arises. Even among those who characterize their religious views as

56

conservative, a majority reject the concept that there are moral absolutes.[8]

These findings suggest that religious faith in America, though widespread, is relatively shallow. However, those Jews and Christians possessed of deep and abiding faith "ground their confidence in reason in the Creator of all reason, and their confidence in understanding in the One who understands everything He made—and loves it, besides."[9]

Elder Dallin H. Oaks has reminded us that "No person with values based on religious beliefs should apologize for taking those values into the public square."[10]

Questions of right or wrong, based on religious *or* secular principles, are therefore legitimate issues for debate on public policy. Abraham Lincoln certainly thought so. In his famous debate with Stephen A. Douglas regarding slavery, Lincoln rejected Douglas's assertion that the national government should allow the majority of voters in a territory to decide whether slavery should be allowed therein. In rebuttal, Lincoln stated, "When Judge Douglas says that whoever, or whatever community, wants slaves, they have a right to have them, he is perfectly logical if there is nothing wrong in the institution; but if you admit that it is wrong, he cannot logically say that anybody has a right to do a wrong."[11]

The Concepts of Justice and Mercy

The concept of justice lies at the bedrock of civilization. Indeed, as Professor Harold J. Berman has pointed out, "At the highest level, surely, the just and the holy are one—or else not only all men but the whole universe, and God Himself, are condemned to an eternal schizophrenia."[12]

Without justice there can be no civilization, only the law of tooth and fang, with victory going to the most powerful. No matter what pressures there are upon us or how much we

57

are misunderstood, no matter the opinions of those in authority, no matter what others say or do, we are all under the judgments of a just God who comprehends perfectly what is right and wrong and knows us better than we know ourselves. These words of the Psalmist come to mind: "Let the floods clap their hands: let the hills be joyful together before the Lord; for he cometh to judge the earth: with righteousness shall he judge the world, and the people with equity" (Psalm 98:8–9).

The knowledge that an all-seeing and all-knowing God will judge us brings both humility and honesty into our lives and our relationships with others. It gives us reason to pause and consider our own motives and examine the possibility that we might, after all, be wrong. It helps us maintain a balance in our lives. It is the enemy of extremism, the ally of moderation.

Old Testament prophets, including Isaiah, Amos, and Micah, proclaimed that God is deeply concerned with how people treat each other. Isaiah wrote, "Cease to do evil; learn to do well; seek judgment, relieve the oppressed, judge the fatherless, plead for the widow" (Isaiah 1:16–17). And Amos proclaimed, "Let judgment run down as waters, and righteousness as a mighty stream" (Amos 5:24). Micah asked, "What doth the Lord require of thee, but to do justly, and to love mercy, and to walk humbly with thy God?" (Micah 6:8). From these teachings flowed the emphasis in Jewish history upon justice and mercy as religious duties. Jesus drew upon that tradition when He said, "Woe unto you, Pharisees! for ye tithe mint and rue and all manner of herbs, and pass over judgment and the love of God" (Luke 11:42).

How grateful we should all be that God is merciful. We are all sinners, and in need of Christ's redeeming grace and

58

the Father's merciful love, as the scriptures and the living prophets attest.

There Is No Public Morality without Private Virtue

The founders of this nation understood that private morality is the fount from whence sound public policy springs. Replying to Washington's first inaugural address, the Senate stated: "We feel, sir, the force and acknowledge the justness of the observation that the foundation of our national policy should be lain in private morality. If individuals be not influenced by moral principles, it is in vain to look for public virtue."[13]

To Whom Much Is Given, of Them Much Is Expected

God has placed a special responsibility on the Latter-day Saints. We have been given more knowledge about sacred things than others have, and ours is the responsibility not only to live the truths entrusted to us but also to convey them to others. President Brigham Young pointed out our unique responsibility as a people and the reason for it: "We have reason to be thankful more than any other people. We have no knowledge of any other people on the face of the earth who possess the oracles of God, the priesthood, and the keys of eternal life. We are in possession of those keys, and, consequently, we are under greater obligations, as individuals and as a community, to work righteousness."[14] Elder Brigham Young Jr. noted our blessings and their attendant responsibilities as follows: "This people are greatly blessed by receiving the Spirit of the Almighty, and by being privileged to go into His house and making covenants with Him, and in return receiving the keys of eternal life from His hands. We are peculiar in this. There is no other people upon the face of the earth that we know anything about who are permitted to make such covenants with the Most High God. If we do not appreciate these blessings it is because we do not live faithfully to the covenants we have made—because we do not do all in our power to fulfill the commandments of the Almighty, and obey, fully and freely, the words and counsels of those who hold God's authority upon the earth, who have led us thus far efficiently, and who can lead us into the presence of our Father and God."[15]

President John Taylor spoke along the same lines:

> It is difficult, as has been remarked, for us sometimes to realize the position we occupy—the relation we sustain to our heavenly Father—the responsibility that rests upon us and the various duties we have to perform in the fulfillment of the purposes of God; in the interest of a world lying in wickedness; in the building up of the Zion of our God, in the establishment of righteousness and in bringing to pass those great and glorious principles which have been contemplated by the Almighty "before the world rolled into existence or the morning stars sang together for joy." It is our lot to be placed upon the earth in this time. It is our lot to have our minds enlightened by the Spirit, intelligence and revelation that flows from God. It is our lot to operate and co-operate with God our heavenly Father,—and with his Son Jesus Christ,—and with the ancient patriarchs, apostles and men of God who have lived before; and while they are operating behind the veil in the interests of humanity in the fulfillment of the purposes of God and in the establishment of righteousness upon the earth, we are here to operate with them, that we and they may act conjointly under the influence and guidance of the Almighty and the power and Spirit of the living God, in carrying out the designs of the great Jehovah. This is what we are here for.[16]

President Joseph F. Smith also reminded us of the need to keep sacred the covenants we make. He said:

> Now, so long as the Latter-day Saints are content to obey the commandments of God, to appreciate the privileges and blessings which they enjoy in the Church, and will use their time, their talents, their substance, in honor to the name of God, to build up Zion, and to establish truth and righteousness in the earth, so long our heavenly Father is bound by His oath and covenant to protect them from every opposing foe, and to help them to overcome every obstacle that can possibly be arrayed against them or thrown in their pathway; but the moment a community begin to be wrapt up in themselves, become selfish, become engrossed in the temporalities of life, and put their faith in riches, that moment the power of God begins to withdraw from them, and if they repent not the Holy Spirit will depart from them entirely, and they will be left to themselves. That which was given them will be taken away, they will lose that which they had, for they will not be worthy of it. God is just as well as merciful, and we need not expect favors at the hand of the Almighty except as we merit them, at least in the honest desires of our hearts, and the desire and intent will not always avail unless our acts correspond.[17]

Change Must Start with the Individual

Make no mistake about it: if the world is to be changed, the change must start with the individual and spread outward to families, communities, and nations.

"When thou art converted, strengthen thy brethren," said Jesus to Peter (Luke 22:32). Conversion begins with self; we cannot change the world until we have changed first ourselves and then those of our own household. We must therefore teach correct principles to our children and grandchildren and practice those principles faithfully in our own lives, recognizing that example is the great teacher.

Jesus, the Great Exemplar

Jesus, the only perfect and sinless man, provides the perfect example for us in all aspects of life. Desiring neither notoriety nor adulation, he had no ego needs at all. He was totally selfless; his only desire was to do the will of God. "I seek not mine own will, but the will of the Father which hath sent me. . . . I am come in my Father's name" (John 3:30, 43).

Yet Jesus knew exactly who he was and his purpose on earth. his selflessness did not lead to lack of self-assurance or reduce his ability to act decisively. At the very beginning of his ministry, he came to Nazareth, "where he had been brought up," and spoke in the synagogue there, quoting from Isaiah, "The Spirit of the Lord is upon me, because he hath anointed me to preach the gospel to the poor; he hath sent me to heal the broken-hearted, to preach deliverance to the captives, and recovering of sight to the blind, to set at liberty them that are bruised, to preach the acceptable year of the Lord" (Luke 4:16–19). Then, closing the book, he intoned these words of power and majesty: "This day is this scripture fulfilled in your ears" (Luke 4:21).

To the Samaritan woman at Jacob's well Jesus spoke of living water, springing up unto everlasting life. The woman, not fully comprehending Jesus' words nor who he was, said to him, "I know that Messias cometh, which is called Christ: when he is come, he will tell us all things." Then came this wondrous reply: "I that speak unto thee am he" (John 4:25–26). The power and majesty of Jesus' words, his total self-assurance, coupled with majestic humility, touch and tug at the heart!

On the cross, drenched not only with the deep physical suffering he was forced to endure but also with the infinitely greater spiritual agony having to do with his atonement for the sins of the world, Jesus thought of others, not of himself. No cry of self-pity escaped his lips, no plea for mercy was heard, indeed, "No mur-m'ring word escaped his tongue" (*Hymns*, no. 191). His thoughts, as always, were turned toward others. To the plea of the repentant thief He responded with these words of comfort, "To day shalt thou be with me in paradise" (Luke 23:43); to his mother, he proclaimed, pointing to John, "Woman, behold thy son!" (John 19:26). His final words were to him who had "sent him to die," "Father, into thy hands I commend my spirit" (Luke 23:46). So majestic is the scene, so tender the feelings it invokes, "I scarce can take it in. . . . Then sings my soul, my Savior God, to thee, How great thou art! How great thou art!" (*Hymns*, no. 86).

The Example of Paul the Apostle

Though no mortal can even approach Christ's glory and majesty, Saul of Tarsus, known to us by his Latin name *Paul*, stands for all time as a great example of total consecration to Christ and his cause. Pierced to the heart by the glory of the resurrected Christ, whom he met and accepted under dramatic circumstances on the Damascus road, Paul wore out his days in "weariness and painfulness," bearing testimony to "great and small" of the Master whom he loved more than life itself, ever grateful to be in the service of the Savior.

For nearly three decades the noble Cilician lived "as it were appointed to death" (1 Corinthians 4:9), reviled, persecuted, defamed, hungry, thirsty, buffeted, with no certain dwelling place (see 1 Corinthians 4:11–12), but glorying always in his testimony of the Savior and his gospel. Oh, how

63

Paul suffered in Christ's cause: "Of the Jews five times received I forty stripes save one. Thrice was I beaten with rods, once was I stoned, thrice I suffered shipwreck, a night and a day I have been in the deep," he wrote of his hardships (2 Corinthians 11:24–25).

Paul's trials and tribulations molded him as clay in the potter's hands, until he became one whose every deed and desire were dedicated to Jesus, "For I determined not to know any thing among you, save Jesus Christ, and him crucified" (1 Corinthians 2:2). Paul longed for only two things—to "preach . . . the unsearchable riches of Christ" (Ephesians 3:8), and then, when his mortal ministry was over, to feel worthy to say, "I have fought a good fight, I have finished my course, I have kept the faith: Henceforth there is laid up for me a crown of righteousness, which the Lord, the righteous judge, shall give me at that day: and not to me only, but unto all them also that love his appearing" (2 Timothy 4:7–8).

One of the saddest statements in all of Paul's writings is found in his second letter to his beloved Timothy. "For Demas hath forsaken me," wrote Paul from Rome, "having loved this present world" (2 Timothy 4:10).

I have often wondered and worried about what happened to Demas. He is mentioned in two of Paul's earlier letters— to the Colossians and to Philemon. He had obviously been a useful and loved companion in the work. Why did he forsake the cause he had once embraced? Did he perhaps tire of the discipline needed for Christian commitment?

Was he overcome by the selfishness of the natural man, and, looking back to old ways and old habits, did he become unfit for the kingdom of God? (See Luke 9:62.) Perhaps he was seduced by one or more of the temptations of the flesh. Certainly Demas did not endure to the end; but losing his grip on the iron rod, he fell away into the dark and filthy

64

torrent of the world. Remembering the Savior's admonition to seek after and bring back the lost lamb, how Paul must have wept and grieved over Demas.

Though our world of the late twentieth century is much different from that in which Paul lived, there are many who represent the modern counterparts of Demas. Having loved too much this present world, thinking more of themselves than of the Savior, they slip away from the Church and kingdom of God, forsaking the sweet and satisfying fruits of fellowship with the Saints for the tinsel and glitter of the world's tawdry counterfeits. With no "deepness of earth" they are soon scorched and wither away (see Matthew 13:5–6). For some such "social saints," the root of the problem is selfishness, an unwillingness to "give away all [their] sins to know [Christ]" (see Alma 22:18).

Blessed Are the Meek

Is there, then, one single attribute of character that best characterizes the man or woman of Christ, enabling him or her to subdue the "natural man"? Some might say *love, courage, faithfulness,* or *integrity.* Without in any way decrying the importance of each of the above, and many others as well, I submit that perhaps the most Christlike of all attributes of character is that of meekness, or in other words, humble submissiveness. Elder Neal A. Maxwell explains why: "Meekness ranks low on the mortal scale of things, yet high on God's: 'For none is acceptable before God, save the meek and lowly in heart' (Moroni 7:44). The rigorous requirements of Christian discipleship are clearly unattainable without meekness. In fact, meekness is needed in order to be spiritually successful, whether in matters of the intellect, in the management of power, in the dissolution of personal pride, or in coping with the challenges of daily life. Jesus, the carpenter—who, with Joseph, 'undoubtedly had experience making yokes'—gave us that marvelous metaphor: 'Take my yoke upon you, and learn of me; for I am meek and lowly in heart.' (Matthew 11:29.) The yoke of obedience to Him is far better than servitude to sin, but the demands are real. . . . Among the qualities to be developed in order to . . . be more like Him and later with Him, is the quality of meekness. It is upon this quality that so many other things, in turn, depend. Without meekness, we cannot accept the gospel, be baptized worthily, maintain our faith, or enjoy the companionship of the Holy Ghost. Without meekness, we cannot retain a remission of our sins, nor can we come to have still further knowledge about Jesus Christ. And, finally, without meekness, we cannot enjoy the highest gospel ordinances worthily."[18]

It hardly needs mentioning that meekness is not the same as servility. He who is meek does not grovel or cringe; he is no milksop. Meekness connotes strength, not weakness. After all, Jesus, the perfect example of meekness, and our model in every way, was the epitome of strength.

But, oh, how meek he was, humbly submissive to his Father's will in all things. To Pilate's query, "Art thou a king then?" Jesus replied with calm majesty: "Thou sayest that I am a king. To this end was I born, and for this cause came I into the world, that I should bear witness unto the truth" (John 18:37). Then he, the creator of worlds without number, who could for the asking have had "more than twelve legions of angels" to come to his aid, went "as a lamb to the slaughter" and was crucified between two malefactors on Golgotha's ghastly hill. None can—or ever will—compare with him. But each of us must try to follow him every day of our lives.

Let Virtue Garnish Your Thoughts

Private virtue is a fabric made up of small threads of goodness that combine to produce the tapestry of a life of integrity. The real heroes and heroines of the world most often go unheralded and unsung. Virtue and its companions, integrity and courage, are found in the everyday decisions and actions of ordinary life. Those worthy of our admiration ought to include the employee who gives a full and honest day's work; the employer who rewards loyalty and service; the craftsman who takes pride in the cunning of his or her hands; the father who cherishes his relationship with his children above life in the fast track; the stay-at-home mother who sees herself not as a second-class citizen but as a partner with God who is privileged to participate in the most difficult and noblest of all human tasks; spouses who are loyal and true to each other through the joys and sorrows of life; the professional who places honesty, honor, and service above the making of money; the corporate executive who sees himself or herself as a steward, not a freebooter. These are they who possess spiritual wholeness and are the real heroes of life.

How glorious and pure are those who live lives of private virtue. They can sleep at night secure in the knowledge that they have done their best. Their consciences are devoid of offense to anyone, their honor unsullied by the sordid compromises and shady dealings of a wicked world. Their values and convictions are clearly fixed and defined and well-known to their associates. They are not for sale, at any price. They seek first the kingdom of God and his righteousness and are little interested in power or wealth. They understand that "a man's life consisteth not in the abundance of the things which he possesseth" (Luke 12:15), and they love people, not things. Others see them as people who can be trusted, men and women of honor and of real substance.

As virtue is built brick by brick from a multitude of little thoughts and actions, so too are most sins seductively small. In his book *The Screwtape Letters,* C. S. Lewis, with his unusual grasp of "things as they really are," has the master devil, Screwtape, instruct his apprentice nephew, Wormwood, in proper devilish tactics: "You will say that these are very small sins; and doubtless, like all young tempters, you are anxious to be able to report spectacular wickedness. . . . It does not matter how small the sins are, provided that their cumulative effect is to edge the man away from the Light and out into the Nothing. . . . Indeed, the safest road to Hell is the gradual one—the gentle slope, soft underfoot, without sudden turnings, without milestones, without signposts."[19]

Beware of the small sins, which bleed us drop by drop from a thousand small cuts, rather than from one single dramatic slash!

7

PROTECTING THE FAMILY

The scriptures tell us that marriage is "ordained of God unto man" (D&C 49:15), and God's modern-day prophets have repeatedly reaffirmed that eternal principle, reminding us that heaven is the origin and continuation of the ideal home and that God intended husband and wife to serve together as full and equal partners in a sacred enterprise of eternal consequence.

"The time will come," said President Spencer W. Kimball, "when only those who believe deeply and actively in the family will be able to preserve their families in the midst of the gathering evil around us."[1] I submit that time is now upon us.

In a solemn proclamation to the world on the family dated 23 September 1995,[2] the First Presidency and the Council of the Twelve Apostles declared that marriage between man and woman is essential to God's eternal plan, and "that successful marriages and families are established and maintained on principles of faith, prayer, repentance, forgiveness, respect, love, compassion, work, and wholesome recreational activities." In fulfilling these sacred responsibilities regarding children, "fathers and mothers are obligated to help one another as equal partners."

Why is it that God has ordained marriage between a man and a woman as the pattern all societies must follow if they are to survive and flourish, a pattern that is the foundation of all human community? Several reasons come to mind.

Human society extends over time; it has a past and a future.

Through the mysterious miracle of our participation in the procreative process, in partnership with God, we transmit life to the next generation, to those who will succeed us. Only in marriage can there be a full and effective expression of the commitment and time necessary to successfully nurture children. In marriage we learn to see ourselves not only as the link with past generations but also as stewards of the future, particularly the future of our children and their children. We see ourselves as an integral part of the great unfolding tapestry of the human race, linked both to the past and the future.

In marriage we learn to value differences.

We learn that male and female complement each other, not only physically and intellectually but also spiritually. There are differences in the natural gifts of men and women. In marriage these differences complement each other to create a divine wholeness. President Spencer W. Kimball pointed out that "in his wisdom and mercy, our Father made men and women dependent on each other for the full flowering of their potential. Because their natures are somewhat different, they can complement each other; because they are in many ways alike, they can understand each other."[3]

Marriage requires the direction and restraint of many impulses, particularly the selfishness of the "natural man" (see Mosiah 3:19).

In marriage we learn to place another person's needs rather than our own desires at the center of life. Our

70

priorities and commitments thus go beyond the demands of self-interest. As we serve our spouse and other family members, we master the selfishness that is the great enemy of spirituality, and in the process we find who we really are and what we can become. The absence of the loving, caring, and mutually supportive relationships found only in marriage and in the family circle leads almost inevitably to the malignant and distorted culture now predominant in many communities, a culture characterized by physical violence, predatory sexual behavior, and social irresponsibility.

Marriage is the school for Zion.[4]

In Zion, divine love, based upon the equal worth of all souls, is the foundation for all laws. Only in the exercise of that divine love may all enjoy the fullness of life and become a Zion people. Marriage for time and all eternity, performed in the holy temple by an officiator endowed with priesthood authority, unites husband and wife in a sacred relationship intended to endure forever. In marriage we learn to be one with another while retaining our own individual identities in full, complete, and equal partnership with our spouse. The true intimacy necessary for the fullness of life can only be achieved within the context of unconditional love and equality between spouses. Roles, of course, differ between spouses, but both are co-equals in the relationship. Each home, then, has the potential to become a small Zion, and from that foundation the city of Zion can be built.

Marriage is the best mechanism to ensure that two parents share in the raising of children.

The lessons of history make this point clear. The best mechanism ever developed to assist in raising children is to have both parents participate in the task. Indeed, it is a divinely conceived concept. "Parents have a sacred duty to rear their children in love and righteousness, to provide for their physical and spiritual needs, . . . Husbands and wives— mothers and fathers—will be held accountable before God for the discharge of these obligations."[5]

The Words of the Prophets

The prophets, whose teachings are increasingly honored more in the breach than the observance, paint a starkly different picture of family life than that espoused by the strident voices of secularism. They teach that marriage is ordained of God as the basic unit in His kingdom. By virtue of the sealing power and by obedience to gospel laws and ordinances, marriage can endure eternally (see D&C 49:15; 132:19). Marriage and family life must be our highest priorities. We must do all in our power to protect, enrich, and preserve them. Fathers and mothers play distinct but complementary roles in establishing and maintaining families. President Spencer W. Kimball summarized the eternal importance of the family and of parents as follows: "The Lord organized the whole program in the beginning with a father who procreates, provides, and loves, and directs, and a mother who conceives and bears and nurtures and feeds, and trains. The Lord could have organized it otherwise but chose to have a unit with responsibility and purposeful associations where children train and discipline each other and come to love, honor, and appreciate each other. The family is the great plan of life as conceived and organized by our Father in Heaven."[6]

His words echo those of a proclamation of the First Presidency and the Quorum of the Twelve Apostles, dated April 6, 1980: "We affirm the sanctity of the family as a divine creation and declare that God our Eternal Father will hold parents accountable to rear their children in light and truth, teaching them 'to pray and to walk uprightly before the Lord' (D&C 68:28). We teach that the most sacred of all relationships, those family associations of husbands and wives and parents and children, may be continued eternally when marriage is solemnized under the authority of the holy priesthood exercised in temples dedicated for these divinely authorized purposes."[7]

In their prophetic declaration on the family dated 23 September 1995, the First Presidency and Council of the Twelve included this somber warning: "We warn that individuals who violate covenants of chastity, who abuse spouse or offspring, or who fail to fulfill family responsibilities will one day stand accountable before God. Further, we warn that the disintegration of the family will bring upon individuals, communities, and nations the calamities foretold by ancient and modern prophets."[8]

Latter-day prophets have spoken plainly about the importance of mothers remaining in their homes to care for their children. Unfortunately much of their counsel has gone unheeded, even by many Latter-day Saint families.

There are, of course, many women with young children who are widowed or divorced or who find themselves in unusual circumstances where they are required to work outside the home. Numerous others, however, are not in that situation. In the words of President Spencer W. Kimball: "Too many mothers work away from home to furnish sweaters and music lessons and trips and fun for their children. Too many women spend their time in socializing, in politicking, in public services when they should be home to teach and train and receive and love their children into security."[9]

The truth of the matter is that mothers are needed in the home to teach moral standards to their children. Elder Boyd K. Packer put it this way: "I would go back to the home that has a mother there. I ask you, what good is the big picture window and the lavish appointments and the priceless door in a home if there is no mother there? The mother as a mother, not a breadwinner, is an essential figure in this battle against immorality and wickedness. I would also go back to the family where children were accountable and where the father was the head of the family. Would you think me naive if I were to propose that this battle ultimately will be won on such simple grounds as the children coming in after school to homemade bread and jam with Mama there?"[10]

Principles to Follow in Teaching Youth

Those responsible for teaching youth may wish to keep the following principles in mind.

Focus first on doctrine, not on errant behavior.

The scriptures tell of the power of the word of God: "And now, as the preaching of the word had a great tendency to lead the people to do that which was just—yea, it had had more powerful effect upon the minds of the people than the sword, or anything else, which had happened unto them—therefore Alma thought it was expedient that they should try the virtue of the word of God" (Alma 31:5).

Elder Boyd K. Packer has reminded us: "The study of the doctrines of the gospel will improve behavior quicker than a study of behavior will improve behavior. Preoccupation with unworthy behavior can lead to unworthy behavior. That is why we stress so forcefully the study of the doctrines of the gospel."[11]

It is especially important that youth be taught the doctrine of the Atonement and helped to see how the Savior's sacrifice and suffering applies to them personally. The best place to teach doctrine is in the home, in family home evening discussions, personal and family scripture study, and, perhaps most importantly, by example.

The basic responsibility to teach youth lies with their parents.

These well-known words of Elder Boyd K. Packer bear repetition:

"If my boy needs counseling, bishop, it should be my responsibility first, and yours second.

"If my boy needs recreation, bishop, I should provide it first, and you second.

"If my boy needs correction, that should be my responsibility first, and yours second.

"If I am failing as a father, help me first, and my children second.

"Do not be too quick to take over from me the job of raising my children.

"Do not be too quick to counsel them and solve all of the problems. Get me involved. It is my ministry."[12]

There are eternal rewards resulting from sexual purity.

They include peace of mind, an unsullied reputation, the presence and help of the Spirit in one's life, a life of worthiness to partake of sacred covenants and holy ordinances, and finally, and most importantly, a life that will qualify us to return to the presence of the Father and his Holy Son.

Sexual impurity is a serious matter.

In instructing his wayward son, Alma counseled Corianton as follows: "And this is not all, my son, Thou didst do that which was grievous unto me; for thou didst forsake the ministry, and did go over into the land of Siron among the borders of the Lamanites, after the harlot Isabel. Yea, she did steal away the hearts of many; but this was no excuse for thee, my son. Thou shouldst have tended to the ministry wherewith thou was entrusted. Know ye not, my son, that these things are an abomination in the sight of the Lord; yea, most abominable above all sins save it be the shedding of innocent blood or denying the Holy Ghost?" (Alma 39:3–5).

There are many aspects to the seriousness of sexual transgression, which youth deserve to be taught in power and plainness. They include the following:

◆ *Difficulty of repentance.* There are many who do not realize how difficult it is to repent, how many tears must be shed, what agony of soul is involved. On this subject President Ezra Taft Benson has said: "I would not have anyone believe that there is no hope if there are some who have made such a grievous mistake, because repentance and forgiveness are also a part of the gospel. Thank God for that! But it must be real repentance. Such repentance is a deep, heartfelt sorrow for sin that produces a reformation of life. It is not just a confession of guilt. Sometimes we regard all too lightly the principle of repentance, thinking that it only means confession, that it only means feeling sorry for ourselves. But it is more than that. It is a deep, burning, and heartfelt sorrow for sin that will drive us to our knees in humility and tears— a deep, heartfelt sorrow for sin that produces a reformation of life. That is the right test: a reformation of life. Only then may the God of heaven in his mercy and his goodness see fit to forgive us. He—not the priesthood on the earth—is the judge. Priesthood holders can only carry out certain requirements. They can require certain things set forth in the revelations, but forgiveness comes from above."[13]

◆ *Sexually transmitted disease.* In addition to devastating diseases that have been around for centuries, the ghastly specter of AIDS now hovers over many relationships. The incidence of AIDS is increasing with fearful rapidity among teenagers. The way to avoid sexually transmitted disease is remarkably simple: total sexual abstinence before marriage and total sexual fidelity within marriage to an equally faithful spouse.

◆ *Unwanted pregnancy.* The consequences of unwanted pregnancy are replayed scores of thousands of times each month in this and every other nation. Of even more serious consequence is the wicked way in which many unwanted pregnancies are taken care of, by abortion.

◆ *Loss of reputation.* Even in today's world, gossip's tongue inevitably touches all involved with sexual impurity. There *are* no secrets. This loss of reputation may jeopardize future relationships with people who have high moral standards.

◆ *Restrictions in missionary service.* "Be ye clean, that bear the vessels of the Lord" (Isaiah 52:11), the scriptures remind us. The First Presidency has pointed out, in an inspired letter to priesthood leaders dated March 4, 1993, that "full-time missionary service is not a right, but a privilege." Only those who are morally clean and worthy to enter the temple may be called to missionary service. Nor should individuals harbor the erroneous supposition they can "sow their wild oats," be profligate for a season, and then after hasty repentance qualify for missionary service. It's not that easy; in certain cases, they may have disqualified themselves permanently from serving as one of the Lord's chosen ambassadors. Do not trifle with sacred things!

◆ Last, but perhaps most importantly, *sexual impurity leads to loss of the companionship of the Spirit.* Without the guidance and direction of the Holy Ghost, we are vulnerable to the buffetings of the adversary and ill-prepared to withstand the temptations and evil of the world.

Each individual, by reason of his or her divine nature, possesses an inherent power to resist temptation.

To the Saints of Corinth, Paul wrote, "There hath no temptation taken you but such as is common to man; but God is faithful, who will not suffer you to be tempted above that ye are able; but will with the temptation also make a way to escape, that ye may be able to bear it" (1 Corinthians 10:13).

◆ In this respect, President Gordon B. Hinckley taught, "That man [woman, boy, girl, child] who knows that he is a child of God, created in the image of a divine Father and gifted with a potential for the exercise of great and godlike virtues, will discipline himself against the sordid, lascivious elements to which all are exposed" (*Ensign,* November 1975, 39).

Our youth today do live in perilous times. Adult purveyors of drugs, violence, and pornography use every means to sell their products to a new generation. The world is too much with us!

◆ Elder Harold B. Lee spoke of the need for all Saints, including youth, to live apart from the world, pointing out the blessings that come to those who have the courage to withstand temptation and live as they should. He said:

Against the daily temptations that come to influence us to live below the standards that we profess and teach, the Lord admonishes us first with a blessing as he has said to his disciples: "Blessed are ye, when men shall revile you, and persecute you, and shall say all manner

78

of evil against you falsely, for my sake . . . for so persecuted they the prophets which were before you"
(Matthew 5:11–12).

And then he warns us: "Woe unto you, when all men
shall speak well of you! for so did their fathers to the
false prophets" (Luke 6:26).

While it becomes us to seek the goodwill of righteous
men and women everywhere, it is well for us to remember that when the lewd, the immoral, and the corrupt
begin to compliment us and to curry favor with us, that
we had better begin to examine ourselves to see if we are
doing our full duty.[14]

Helping Youth to Be Strong

What are the keys to helping youth live righteously in a
world full of sin? They include the following:

**All youth need to have a personal experience of
healthy, loving, appropriate relationships.**

◆ Teens need to feel the love of their parents. When trust and
love exist, teens welcome counsel. Siblings, other family
members, friends, and Church leaders can also provide
both love and counsel.

◆ Teens learn much about appropriate behavior by observing
appropriate loving relationships of affection and mutual
respect between their parents.

◆ Parents must set the example by their own behavior. As one
of the parents of a young person surveyed in the Bowman
Gray study cited previously (pp. 8–10) said, "I think if we
want to teach responsible behavior to our teens, the responsible behavior must begin with ourselves."

These words of scripture come to mind: "And again, inasmuch as parents have children in Zion, or in any of her stakes which are organized, that teach them not to understand the doctrine of repentance, faith in Christ the Son of the living God, and of baptism and the gift of the Holy Ghost by the laying on of the hands, when eight years old, the sin be upon the heads of the parents. For this shall be a law unto the inhabitants of Zion, or in any of her stakes which are organized. And their children shall be baptized for the remission of their sins when eight years old, and receive the laying on of the hands. And they shall also teach their children to pray, and to walk uprightly before the Lord" (D&C 68:25–28).

Teenagers need to experience a feeling of self-efficacy, a feeling their lives are under control.

◆ Young people need experience and confidence in making and putting into effect sound decisions, thereby building their feelings of self-reliance and self-respect.

◆ One of the best ways teenagers gain a feeling of self-efficacy is through work—not mindless drudgery, of course, but meaningful work, which makes them think, make decisions, *and* sweat.

Teenagers need a clear statement of standards they are expected to follow.

◆ The scriptures and our prophet-leaders have set out clearly the standards of morality to which all—youth and adults— must adhere if their behavior is to be acceptable to God. President Ezra Taft Benson gave this advice to our precious youth: "Do not be misled by Satan's lies. There is no lasting happiness in immorality. There is no joy to be found in

80

breaking the law of chastity. Just the opposite is true. There may be momentary pleasure. For a time it may seem like everything is wonderful. But quickly the relationship will sour. Guilt and shame set in. We become fearful that our sins will be discovered. We must sneak and hide, lie and cheat. Love begins to die. Bitterness, jealousy, anger, and even hate begin to grow. All of these are the natural results of sin and transgression.

"On the other hand, when we obey the law of chastity and keep ourselves morally clean, we will experience the blessings of increased love and peace, greater trust and respect for our marital partners, deeper commitment to each other, and therefore a deep and significant sense of joy and happiness.

"We must not be misled into thinking these sins are minor or that consequences are not that serious."[15]

President Thomas S. Monson added these words of wise counsel: "Because sexual intimacy is so sacred, the Lord requires self-control and purity before marriage, as well as full fidelity after marriage. In dating, treat your date with respect, and expect your date to show that same respect for you. Tears inevitably follow transgression. Men, take care not to make women weep, for God counts their tears."[16]

With parental support, guidance and encouragement, youth should scrupulously follow the standards set by the Brethren.

The booklet *For the Strength of Youth* (The Church of Jesus Christ of Latter-day Saints, 1990) is a precious guide for teenagers and their parents. Parents and youth should read and discuss it together.

From my own experience as a father and as a counselor

of youth, I believe the following standards are worthy of special emphasis:

◆ *No early dating.* There is great wisdom in the standard given by the Brethren: "Do not date until you are sixteen years old."

◆ *Date people with high standards.* This advice from *For the Strength of Youth* provides assurance both for anxious parents and teenagers: "Date only those who have high standards, who respect your standards, and in whose company you can maintain the standards of the gospel of Jesus Christ."

◆ *Parents should meet and become acquainted with their children's dates.* I have a friend, the father of several vivacious, beautiful teenaged daughters, who insisted that he meet and, yes, approve of the young men who came to take his daughters out on dates. "I wouldn't let a young man take my new car out for an evening's driving unless I knew his name and something about his honesty and integrity," he assured me, "so why should I let him take my daughter, who is infinitely more precious?"

As an extension of the above, wise parents take the time to become acquainted with their children's friends. They know where their children are and, without being intrusive or stifling, keep tabs on their whereabouts. And they don't wait until their children are teenagers to start doing so. If you don't know where your child is at age eight, how likely are you to know where he or she is at eighteen?

◆ *Be scrupulous in observance of the Word of Wisdom.* The association between drug use, including alcohol and marijuana, and sexual activity is so strong it cannot be ignored. By lowering inhibitions and dulling the conscience, drug use may lead to immoral behavior.

Combating Street Gangs

We turn now to the terrible scourge of criminal street gangs. What can we do, as parents and citizens, to combat them? Part of the answer, at least in the short-term, lies with aggressive law enforcement. But much more is involved. In speaking of the declining values in our society, which lie at the root of the gang problem, President Gordon B. Hinckley, with prophetic wisdom has noted: "Those who are concerned with the problem advocate more legal regulation, large appropriations for increased police forces, tax increases to build additional jails and prisons. These may be needed to deal with the present problems. They may help in the near term. But they will be only as a bandage too small for the sore. They may help in taking care of the fruits, but they will not get at the roots. In searching for remedies, we speak of a greater work that must be done in our schools. But educators have largely abdicated their responsibility for teaching values. The Church is looked to—this and all other churches. I am grateful for what the Pope recently said in Denver in warning against moral pitfalls. I am pleased to note that the Baptists have begun a campaign for chastity. We as a church are doing much, very much, and I think we are accomplishing much. But it is not enough.

"When all is said and done, the primary place in building a value system is in the homes of the people."[17]

Prevention, then, must start at home. Recent studies on risk-focused prevention have identified three risk factors within the family which increase the likelihood of violent behavior in children. Violence and gangs are of course inextricably connected.[18] The factors are:

Poor Family Management Practices, including the absence of clear expectations and standards for children's behavior, excessively severe or inconsistent punishment, and parental failure to monitor their children's activities, whereabouts, or friends;

Family Conflict, either between parents or between parents and children, which enhances the risk for violent behavior;

Favorable Parental Attitudes toward and Involvement in Violent Behavior, which increases the risk that children witnessing violence will act violently themselves.

Other factors also increase the likelihood youth will engage in violence. As outlined by Hawkins, they include the following social conditions:

Neighborhoods

Availability of Guns

A teenager with ready access to firearms through family, friends, or a source on the street, is at increased risk of violence.

Community Laws or Norms Favorable to Crime

Social practices often send conflicting messages to young people. If school officials or parents promote "just say no" themes while abusing alcohol and other drugs themselves, teenagers quickly discern the hypocrisy involved and are turned off by it.

Media Portrayals of Violence

Despite Hollywood's protestations to the contrary, three decades of research show there is a clear connection between repeated depictions of violence and the development of aggressive and violent behavior.

Community Disorganization

Indifference to cleanliness and orderliness, high rates of vandalism, little surveillance of public places by neighborhood residents, and an absence of parental involvement in schools, are indications of a community with a reduced sense of organization and attachment. In such places a sense of pride in belonging to a community is lacking.

Extreme Economic Deprivation

Children who live in deteriorating neighborhoods characterized by extreme poverty are more likely to develop problems with delinquency, teen pregnancy, dropping out of school, and violence. By extension, they are more vulnerable to the attraction of street gangs.

Schools

Antisocial behavior that manifests itself as early as kindergarten through third grade is often an indicator of violent behavior that will surface during adolescence. Misbehaving in class, displaying a defiant attitude, and getting into frequent fights are signals that must not be ignored.

Persistent academic failure in the late elementary grades also puts a youngster at risk. The attendant loss of self-esteem and self-confidence can result in belligerent behavior, which in many cases is an effort to compensate for a sense of inadequacy. It is the *experience* of failing and not a lack of ability *per se* that promotes the violence. Lacking positive peer pressure, parental support, or an understanding teacher or some other mentor, the young person is left to find his or her own troubled way, which is too often marked by recurring violent behavior.

Peer Groups

Young people who associate with peers who engage in antisocial behavior such as drug abuse, delinquency, sexual activity, or violence are much more likely to do the same. The earlier in life this occurs, the greater the likelihood of prolonged, serious, and chronic involvement. (My mother's advice to stay away from inappropriate friends was right!)

Hawkins also points out that there are protective factors that reduce the impact of negative risk factors by providing positive ways a person can respond to them. They include the following:

Morally uplifting beliefs and standards.

The gospel of Christ and the teachings of the Church provide the basis for such beliefs and standards, but they also should include demands for good performance in school and consistent disapproval of problem behavior.

Positive relationships with family members, teachers, or other adults.

For many young people a positive relationship with an admired parent, sibling, uncle, grandmother, teacher, bishop, quorum advisor, etc. can make all the difference. For this to take place three conditions must be met:

- The young person must be given an opportunity for active involvement, a chance to participate consistently and appropriately.
- The young person must have the skills needed to succeed. This requires wise, consistent teaching.
- There must be a consistent system of recognition or reinforcement for doing the right thing. Praise is a powerful aid to the development of self-esteem.

It is instructive to note the views of gang members themselves. Thirty Salt Lake City gang members were recently invited to participate in a think tank in which the young toughs were asked what should be done to help other youth avoid gang involvement. They came up with the following ideas:[19]

- Teach youth early that gangs are bad. According to the youth, parents should be doing this for children between the ages of six and eleven.

- Youth need punishment for bad behavior and rewards for good behavior. Youth want stricter enforcement for offenses. They are concerned that juveniles commit too many crimes before consequences are imposed. They feel detention centers and corrections facilities should be more punitive. They want judges to hand down stricter sentences earlier. The punishment should fit the crime.

- Kids need a safe place to share their feelings and where kids from different gangs can learn to get along together.

- Families need to spend time together. The youth had definite ideas about their expectations of parents. They stated that good parents provide food, clothes, and shelter; they help youth with homework or problems at school; they talk to youth about all sorts of problems (sex, money, medical, etc.); they provide consequences when youth break the rules; they offer encouragement; and they believe in their children. Several youth expressed gratitude that their parents had never given up on them, no matter what they had done.

- Kids need other adults (besides parents) in their lives who care about them and make a difference. Qualities named that were important in these adults included: cares about the youth, works with the

87

parents, talks and listens to the youth, is fair, has free time to spend with the youth, gives warning before punishment, rewards good work, has a sense of humor, makes the youth feel important. Influential people in the lives of youth include teachers, religious leaders, coaches, neighbors, family members, tutors, mentors, etc.

- There need to be more opportunities for youth to succeed in education, including tutoring, scholarships, and getting parents involved.

- Youth want more opportunities to get a job. They also want to know how to get a job, what employers are looking for, and how to do well at work.

- Youth felt stronger efforts should be made to get guns off the streets.

- Youth want to be needed in the community. They want to be involved in making the community a better place. They often feel that adults look down on them and treat them as though they're from a different planet. Youth want to belong.

It seems clear from the above that although street gangs represent a scourge on our society, the means are available to us to reclaim our communities and to refuse to be held hostage to outlaw elements. The task of doing so starts in the home; it is one in which all citizens must share if we are to succeed. It was the English philosopher Edmund Burke who reminded us of our duty by saying, "The only thing necessary for the triumph of evil is for good men to do nothing."

Strengthening Fathers: The Prophets Speak

The prophets of God speak plainly about the importance of fatherhood. They teach men that marriage and family life must be our highest priority and that we must do all in our power to enrich and preserve those institutions. The prophets proclaim that fathers and mothers have essential, distinct, and complementary roles in the cooperative work of establishing and maintaining families. They remind us that the family, with both father and mother present, is the basic unit in the kingdom of God. By virtue of the sealing power exercised by the priesthood, and by faithful continuance in obedience to God's laws and sacred ordinances, families may endure forever. "That same sociality which exists among us here will exist among us there" (D&C 130:2), assuming, of course, that we have lived worthy to receive such ineffable blessings.

In one of his last general addresses as president of The Church of Jesus Christ of Latter-day Saints, President Howard W. Hunter spoke to priesthood bearers on the responsibility they have to be a righteous husband and father.[20] His comments on the four traditional roles of fathers—to be caretaker and protector, moral educator, head of family, and breadwinner—are eminently worthy of repetition. They represent a primer for men everywhere.

Father As Caretaker and Protector

"A righteous father protects his children with his time and presence in their social, educational, and spiritual activities and responsibilities. Tender expressions of love and affection toward children are as much the responsibility of the father as the mother. Tell your children you love them."

Father As Moral Educator

"Take seriously your responsibility to teach the gospel to your family through regular family home evening, family prayer, devotional and scripture reading time, and other teaching moments. Give special emphasis to preparation for missionary service and temple marriage. As patriarch in the home, exercise your priesthood through performing the appropriate ordinances for your family and by giving blessings to your wife and children."

Father As the Head of Family

"Of necessity there must be in the Church and in the home a presiding officer (see D&C 107:21). By divine appointment, the responsibility to preside in the home rests upon the priesthood holder (see Moses 4:22). The Lord intended that the wife be a helpmeet for man (*meet* means equal)—that is, a companion equal and necessary in full partnership. Presiding in righteousness necessitates a shared responsibility between husband and wife; together you act with knowledge and participation in all family matters. For a man to operate independently of or without regard to the feelings and counsel of his wife in governing the family is to exercise unrighteous dominion. . . . You are to love your wife as Christ loved the Church and gave himself for it (see Ephesians 5:25–31)."

Father As Breadwinner

"You who hold the priesthood have the responsibility, unless disabled, to provide temporal support for your wife and children. No man can shift the burden of responsibility to another, not even to his wife. The Lord has commanded that women and children have claim on their husbands and fathers for their maintenance (see D&C 83; 1 Timothy 5:8). . . . Men who abandon their family and fail to meet their responsibility to care for those they have fathered may find their eligibility for a temple recommend and their standing in the Church in jeopardy."

President Hunter's prophetic counsel needs no amplification, clarification, or expansion. If we in this and other nations are to overcome the curse of fatherlessness, which blights our societies, we must do as God and his holy prophets have commanded. In particular, men must learn to act as sons of God rather than as "natural" men who are the enemies of God. As *real* men, not simply as males, they must honor women; nurture, love, and care for their children; and stop excusing the gross sins, which, in Elder Neal A. Maxwell's felicitous phrase, "arise ominously and steadily out of the swamp of self-indulgence and self-pity. . . . Real, personal sacrifice . . . is a willingness to put the animal in us upon the altar and [let] it be consumed."[21]

Faithful Latter-day Saint fathers, however, have a key responsibility in addition to these, which God requires of fathers everywhere. Latter-day Saint fathers, if they are true to the sacred covenants they have made, bear the awesome responsibility of the priesthood of God. With this priesthood they have the power and authority to bless their families and others. Elder John A. Widtsoe stated, "Every father having children born to him under the covenant, is to them as a patriarch, and he has the right to bless his posterity in the authority of the priesthood which he holds."[22] President James E. Faust has noted: "The natural leaders of the family unit are the parents, standing side by side as equals in their loving guidance of their children. Each parent brings a separate enriching influence. *The power of the priesthood should be the dominant influence in family affairs.* Priesthood blessings do not just involve men. They bless equally and fully the women and children of the family."[23] Men who bear God's holy priesthood are under divine obligation to use it to bless others, including most especially the members of their own family.

8

BUILDING A COMMUNITY
OF BELIEVERS

God's prophets, both ancient and modern, put great
stress on the family as a vitally important vehicle for the
development and expression of personal purity. In their
recent proclamation to the world on the family, the First
Presidency and the Council of the Twelve Apostles stated that
"the family is central to the Creator's plan for the eternal destiny of His children. . . . The family is ordained of God. . . .
Happiness in family life is most likely to be achieved when
founded upon the teachings of the Lord Jesus Christ. . . . The
disintegration of the family will bring upon individuals, communities, and nations the calamities foretold by ancient and
modern prophets."

Without in any way diminishing the importance of individuals and families, it must be noted that people also live in
communities. One dictionary defines community as "a body
of people having common organization or interests, or living
in the same place under the same laws and regulations."[1]
Obviously, "community" is different than "congregation,"
which has been defined as "a body of persons met for the
worship of God and for religious instruction." People are by
nature social beings whose lives and feelings are eternally
connected to and intertwined with those of others. For
members of The Church of Jesus Christ of Latter-day Saints,

community is an essential and eternal part of life in this world and throughout the eternities. Individuals reach their full potential only in association and community with others.

Elder Erastus Snow, who played an important role in Latter-day Saint settlement of the Intermountain West, understood the importance of community in its relationship to the family and the individual. He said: "What man, however good be his desires, can control himself and his family in their habits and manners of life and fashions, without the aid of the surrounding community? What sensible man can hold me or my brethren responsible, in all respects, either for ourselves or our households, unaided by the community or while the community are all working against us? But when the community learn to work together, and are agreed in a common purpose, what is it that they can not accomplish? Union is strength."[2]

This concept of mutual interdependence is well-illustrated by the following words, which John Winthrop, later the first governor of the colony of Massachusetts, read to fellow Puritans aboard the *Arbella* on their voyage to what has evolved into the United States of America: "We must be knit together in this work as one. . . . We must delight in each other, make other's conditions our own, rejoice together, mourn together, labour and suffer together . . . as members of the same body."[3]

At the same time, however, each person must retain his or her own individual autonomy. The distinctiveness— indeed, the uniqueness—and independence of "the one" are essential for the health of the community. The reverse of course is also true. Healthy communities are required for the full health of individuals. Communities that do not recognize the sanctity of the individual, that treat people only as a means to further some supposedly greater good and melt all into the lowest common denominator, destroy individuality and quickly become tyrannical and coercive.

It is no exaggeration to say that as the family is to the individual, so too is the community to the family. *Families* nurture and strengthen *individuals,* providing the setting and vehicle for them to grow physically, emotionally, and spiritually. The family protects individuals, particularly the young, who are most vulnerable to forces that adversely affect their health and well-being. Families aid in the development and maintenance of the intellectual, emotional, and spiritual strength of all, particularly children.

So, too, do *communities* nurture *families,* providing a setting within which they can become or stay strong. Families are both protected and assisted by strong communities. Strong community organizations, including churches and schools, supplement and complement the efforts of parents, making not only their work easier but often making the difference between success and failure. Without denying in any way the importance of the family, the old African proverb that it takes a village to raise a child has much truth to it.

If experience shows the validity of the assertion that it is much easier to raise and maintain strong families if the community also is strong, the reverse is also true. It is much more difficult for families to succeed if the community is run-down, crime-ridden, and unsafe. If adults do not care about children, if children are daily exposed to sights and behaviors that frighten and threaten them, and if young people have constantly before them examples of evil and wrongdoing, these things will eventually twist and blight their lives. How difficult it is for a child in many innercity settings in this nation to grow up normally, regardless of what his or her family struggles to accomplish. The streets too often are unsafe. In many places people dare not venture out after dark but lock their doors and pray they will survive the night. When there are few jobs, and unemployed youth congregate on street corners with little to do, it provides many opportunities to get into trouble. Drug and alcohol abuse, drug trafficking, sexual promiscuity, illegitimacy, and crimes of all sorts are the offspring of idleness and too little supervision. The wickedness of the streets is a potent teacher of the young.

Of course, there are exceptions to the general rule that strong communities are needed if we are to have strong families. Just as some strong individuals survive life in severely dysfunctional families, so too some families do well even in severely dysfunctional communities. But the odds are much against such happening.

Let us, then, briefly discuss the significance of community. In his recent and important book, Rodney Stark, perhaps the leading sociologist of religion in North America, provides deep insight into the growth of the Christian community from the time Christianity rose from obscurity to become a world faith.[4] Many factors, of course, were involved, not all of which apply to conditions in our day, but some apply directly to the growth of the worldwide community of Latter-day Saints in the closing years of the twentieth century. An examination of factors influencing the growth of the first Christian communities in light of our needs today thus seems useful. Furthermore, because The Church of Jesus Christ of Latter-day Saints is a revelatory restoration of the Church established by Christ and led by his apostles in the meridian of time, it is relevant to consider the realities of today in light of what transpired in the early Church. I say that in full recognition of the fact that following the death and resurrection of Jesus, and the subsequent death of the apostles, the early Church, bereft of apostolic leadership, eventually lost its way and entered a long, dark night of apostasy. Despite that, there is ample evidence that in the first few centuries after Christ there was a strong sense of community amongst Christians. This should not surprise us, given the differences between Christians and the other inhabitants of the pagan world in which they lived.

Stark mentions the following factors as being significant in the growth of the early Christian community. Their application to our time is shown by illustrations drawn from Latter-day Saint history.

Love and Charity toward Others

A great epidemic, perhaps of measles, swept through the Roman Empire around 260 A.D. Millions died and society was in chaos.[5] In the midst of it all, unlike the pagan peoples around them, who fled for their lives, abandoning the stricken, the Christians distinguished themselves by caring for the sick and dying.

To care for the sick was to many Christians a sacred religious responsibility, something to be embraced, not shunned. Dionysius, a Christian bishop of Alexandria, wrote of the heroic efforts of Christians to care for and comfort others during the terrible plague: "Most of our brother Christians showed unbounded love and loyalty, never sparing themselves and thinking only of one another. Heedless of danger, they took charge of the sick, attending to their every need and ministering to them in Christ, and with them departed this life serenely happy; for they were infected by others with the disease, drawing on themselves the sickness of their neighbors and cheerfully accepting their pains. Many, in nursing and curing others, transferred their death to themselves and died in their stead. . . . The best of our brothers lost their lives in this manner, a number of presbyters, deacons, and laymen winning high commendation so that death in this form, the result of great piety and strong faith, seems in every way the equal of martyrdom."[6]

A century later, the Roman Emperor Julian attempted to institute pagan charities in an effort to match the Christians. Stating that pagans needed to equal the virtues of Christians, he complained that recent growth in the numbers of Christians was caused by "their moral character, even if pretended," and "by their benevolence toward strangers and care for the graves of the dead."[7]

Tertullian, another early Christian leader, who was born of pagan parents in the latter half of the second century, wrote: "It is our care of the helpless, our practice of loving kindness that brands us in the eyes of many of our opponents. 'Only look,' they say, 'Look how they love one another!'"[8]

The exercise of love and charity toward others, including those not of the household of faith, was and still is a central characteristic of Christian communities. The Prophet Joseph Smith understood this principle and taught it repeatedly. "Let the Saints remember that great things depend on their individual exertion, and that they are called to be co-workers with us and the Holy Spirit in accomplishing the great work of the last days; and in consideration of the extent, the blessings and glories of the same, *let every selfish feeling be not only buried, but annihilated; and let love to God and man predominate, and reign triumphant in every mind, that their hearts may become like unto Enoch's of old.*"[9]

On another occasion the Prophet Joseph spoke of the obligations of "a man of property" as follows: "He is to feed the hungry, to clothe the naked, to provide for the widow, to dry up the tear of the orphan, to comfort the afflicted, whether in this church, or in any other, or in no church at all, wherever he finds them."[10]

Saints throughout the ages have followed the Savior's admonition to love one another, to appreciate and care for each other. No community can long exist without such feelings of love and charity, expressed through service to others. The example of love and mutual concern shown for each other by Latter-day Saint pioneer families inspires us all, points us to higher levels of personal performance, and helps us avoid the problems found in our deteriorating contemporary society. Consider the love shown in these extracts from the diary of Patience Loader, a young Englishwoman who traveled across the plains with family members as part of the Martin Handcart Company of 1856.*

> I remember on one occasion when we was camping on the Sweet Water [some] breathren came to our tent and ask us girls to go to there camp and sing for them again. My dear Mother told them she thought we had better not go to sing that night. It made us still more hungary to sing and we had nothing to eat after we came back to the tent. They fealt sorrey for us but thay could not give us anything for thay was short of provisions themselvs untill thay got suplys from home. That night was a terrable cold night. The wind was blowing and the snow drifted into the tent onto our quilts. That morning we had nothing to eat if we got up not untill we could get our small quantity of flour. Poor Mother called to me come Patience get up and make us afiar. I told her that I did not feel like getting up it was so cold and I was not feeling very well. So she ask my sister Tamar to get up and she said she was not well and she could not get up. Then she sais come Maria you get up and she was feeling bad and said that she could not get

* The original spelling has been retained.

up. With this Mother says come girls this will not do. I believe I will have to dance to you and try to make you feel better. Poor dear Mother. She started to sing and dance to us and she slipt down as the snow was frozen and in a moment we was all up to help our dear Mother up for we was afraid she was hurt. She laugh and said I thought I could soon make you all jump up if I danced to you. Then we found that she fell down purposely for she knew we would all get up to see if she was hurt. She said that she was afraid her girls was going to give out and get disscuraged and she said that would never do to give up. We none of us had ever fealt so weak as we did that morning. My dear Mother had kept up wonderfull all through the journey. Before she left England she had been in delicate health. For many years she had not been able to walk amile and after we started on our journey to Utah she was able to walk all across the plains only some times we put her on the hand cart to rest her alittle.

After We left the Sweet Water whare we campt for nine days she was able to ride in the wagon. We was so glad to get Mother in the wagon. If we girls could not ride it did us good to know that Mother could get arest and not have to walk in the snow any more.[11]

Love, mutual concern, and compassion extended beyond the family circle in pioneer society. An episode that occurred in the journey of the first handcart company to arrive in Salt Lake City in 1856 tells us much of the sense of community, which was so strong among the pioneers. An entry in the diary of Archer Walters, an English carpenter, handcart repairman, and coffinmaker sets the stage for the story. It reads as follows: "July 2nd. Brother Parker's little boy, age six, was lost. The father went back to hunt him."[12]

The story is elaborated in the history of the Parker family. Robert and Ann Parker were traveling in McArthur's handcart company with their four children: Max, twelve; Martha Alice, ten; Arthur, five; and Ada, one year old. One day, while the company was passing through a wooded area of Nebraska, little Arthur, fevered and ill, sat down to rest, unnoticed by the other children. A sudden storm came up and the company hurriedly made camp. After a time it was noticed that Arthur was not with the other children, and an organized search for him was begun with no success. The search continued a second day, still without success. The captain, who had no other choice, ordered the company to move on. Food was in short supply and not another day could be lost. Better to lose one than to risk losing many.

"Ann Parker pinned a bright shawl about the thin shoulders of her husband and sent him back alone on the trail to search again for their child. If he found him dead he was to wrap him in the shawl; if alive, the shawl would be a flag to signal her. Ann and her children took up their load and struggled on with the company, while Robert retraced the miles of forest trail, calling, and searching and praying for his helpless little son. At last he reached a mail and trading station where he learned that his child had been found and cared for by a woodsman and his wife. He had been ill from exposure and fright. God had heard the prayers of his people.

"Out on the trail each night Ann and her children kept watch and, when, on the third night the rays of the setting sun caught the glimmer of a bright red shawl, the brave little mother sank in a pitiful heap in the sand. Completely exhausted, Ann slept for the first time in six long days and nights."[13]

In his diary, Archer Walters, the English carpenter previously mentioned, penned this poignant statement, "July 5. Brother Parker brings into camp his little boy that had been lost. Great joy through the camp. The mother's joy I can not describe."[14]

How much emotion, how much heartfelt thanks to God, how much brotherly love and concern, how much sense of community are encompassed in that simple sentence: "Great joy through the camp."

The pioneers shared in each others' joys and sorrows. They wept and rejoiced together, sharing both the good and bad of life. Theirs was a brotherhood and sisterhood, a sense of community, that transcended ethnicity, age, or their mutual trials and suffering. In our world of transient relationships and too much concern about self to the exclusion of others, we would do well to learn from the pioneers' noble examples.

Shared Faith Springing from Deeply Held Religious Beliefs

William H. McNeill has pointed out: "Another advantage Christians enjoyed over pagans was that the teachings of their faith made life meaningful even amid sudden and surprising death. Release from suffering was, after all, much to be desired, in principle if not always in practice. Moreover, even a shattered remnant of survivors who had somehow made it through war or pestilence or both could find warm, immediate and healing consolation in the vision of a heavenly existence for those missing relatives and friends who had died as good Christians. God's omnipotence made life meaningful in time of disaster as well as in time of prosperity; indeed untoward and unexpected disaster, shattering pagan pride and undermining secular institutions, made God's hand more evident than it was in quiet times. Christianity was, therefore, a system of thought and feeling thoroughly

102

adapted to a time of troubles in which hardship, disease, and violent death commonly prevailed."[15]

Cyprian, Bishop of Carthage, writing in 251 A.D. during a terrible plague, noted that tribulation and trials are a time of testing, of schooling for the soul. "How suitable, how necessary it is that this plague and pestilence which seems horrible and deadly, searches out the justice of each and every one and examines the minds of the human race; whether the well care for the sick, whether relatives dutifully love their kinsmen as they should, whether masters show compassion for their ailing slaves, whether physicians do not desert the afflicted. . . . Although this mortality has contributed nothing else, it has especially accomplished this for Christians and servants of God, that we have begun gladly to seek martyrdom while we are learning not to fear death. These are trying exercises for us, not deaths; they give to the mind the glory of fortitude; by contempt of death they prepare for the crown. . . . [O]ur brethren who have been freed from the world by the summons of the Lord should not be mourned, since we know that they are not lost but sent before; that in departing they lead the way; that as travellers, as voyagers are wont to be, they should be longed for, not lamented . . . and that no occasion should be given to pagans to censure us deservedly and justly, on the ground that we grieve for those who we say are living."[16]

Based on their deep belief in Christ and his cause, the early Christians discovered a joy that is a thousand times better than any pleasure of this sinful world. They were despised and persecuted, but they cared not. Their faith sustained them, even unto death. That same view of life's trials as a test of discipleship and a measure of faith is shown in the lives of the early Mormon pioneers. Though many of those called by Church leaders to colonize remote regions of the

ROLLING BACK THE DARKNESS

Intermountain West were surprised, shocked or even thrown into momentary despair, they went anyway. Consider the experience of Robert Gardner, whose journal entry of 1861* tells much of the man and his devotion:

"Sunday the Bishop of my ward Ruben Miller and this other counseler Bro. Alexander Hill (for I was one of his counselers) came to my place on a visit and I took them round my farm and place and the Bishop made the remark. I am glad to See you so wel[l] recovered from being broke up. You ar[e] nerly as well of[f] as you was before you lost your property and went on your mision[.] (He served a mission to Canada in 1857.) My reply was yes I was well of[f] once and it all went of[f] and I am almos[t] afraid of another call[.]

"Sure enough in a few hours some of my nabours who had been to meeting at Salt Lake, caled in and told me that my name was amongst a number of names who were caled today to go South on a mision to make a new Setelment and rase cotten and Start right away."

And then descriptively he recorded his reaction to the news:

"I looked and Spit[,] took of[f] my hat and Scratched and thought and. said allright[.]

"Next day I went up to the city and Seen George A. Smith in the historians office[.] He lafed when I went in and Said dont blame anyone but me[.] The President told me to get up a list of names Sutable for that misson So I thought of you got one and thought you would be willing to go if caled[.] So I put your name down."

But the door was left open for Gardner, who later became a bishop in St. George, to turn down the call. The colorful pioneer recorded the comments of Elder Smith, who later

* Original spelling and punctuation retained.

104

became a counselor to President Young: "But if you dont want to go Step to the Presidents office and ask him to take your name of[f] the list and he will do it."

Brother Gardner replied, "I Said I expect he would but shant try him."[17]

A People of One Heart and One Mind

Stark points out that "in uniting its empire, Rome created economic and political unity at the cost of cultural chaos. People of many cultures, speaking many languages, worshiping all manner of gods, had been dumped together helter-skelter. Christianity served as a revitalization movement that arose in response to the misery, chaos, fear and brutality of life in the urban Greco-Roman world. To cities filled with the homeless and impoverished, Christianity offered charity as well as hope. To cities filled with newcomers and strangers, Christianity offered an immediate basis for attachments. To cities filled with orphans and widows, Christianity provided a new and expanded sense of family. To cities torn by violent ethnic strife, Christianity offered a new basis for social solidarity. And to cities faced with epidemics, fires, and earthquakes, Christianity offered effective housing services."[18]

Early Latter-day Saint pioneers also developed a distinctive culture by submerging their many ethnic and cultural differences into a broader, gospel-based world view. Elder Erastus Snow, whose Cotton Mission in St. George succeeded the Iron Mission in Parowan and Cedar City, noted: "We found a Scotch party, a Welch party, an English party, and an American party, and we turned Iron Masters and undertook to put all these parties through the furnace, and run out a party of Saints for building up the Kingdom of God."[19] As Noel B. Reynolds has pointed out: "The gospel is essentially subversive of the world views perpetuated by the cultures of man; for the gospel does have its own world view, teaching men that everything in this world was created by God, that men themselves are spiritual beings and spirit children of their Father in heaven, and that obedience to his commandments as received through personal revelation takes priority over any requirements of a traditional culture."[20]

Close Attachments to Each Other

Early Christian communities grew rapidly, in part, so Stark notes,[21] because they spread through preexisting social networks. He believes that "typically, people do not *seek* a new religious faith; they *encounter* one through their ties to other people who already accept this faith. This pattern has the potential for much faster growth than the one-by-one conversion of social isolates."[22] Furthermore, "religious movements can grow because their members continue to form new relationships with outsiders."

Stark concludes that "the primary source of Mormon converts is along network lines. The average convert was preceded into the church by many friends and relatives. It is network growth that so distinguishes the Mormon rate of growth—meanwhile, other contemporary religious movements will count their growth in thousands, not millions, for lack of a network pattern of growth."

Interestingly, Stark believes that the early Christian church must have grown at the rate of about forty percent per decade for the first three-and-one-half centuries, in order for it to have succeeded as it did in becoming a world faith. This figure, he notes, is close to the average growth rate of forty-three percent per decade that The Church of Jesus Christ of Latter-day Saints has maintained over the past century. My own calculations for the decade 1985–1995 indicate that the Church grew by an astounding fifty-eight percent during that ten-year period. I thank God that The Church of Jesus Christ of Latter-day Saints has always been a missionary church, seeking to obey the Savior's admonition to go "into all the world, and preach the gospel to every creature" (Mark 16:15).

I have come to understand that the benefits of missionary work come not only to those who are baptized by authority but also to those who are the baptizers. Missionary work is the lifeblood of the Church, not only because it provides a continual influx of new and enthusiastic converts but because it is essential for the continual spiritual growth of those already in the fold. Churches without a vibrant and growing missionary effort simply wither and die over time.

Close attachments to each other were particularly strong in pioneer Latter-day Saint communities in the Intermountain West. In contradiction to the usual pattern of settlement of the American West, generally speaking, Latter-day Saints congregated in villages, going out to their surrounding farms each day to work the land. Several hundred villages, each remarkably like the next one, were established in the first half century of Mormon colonization. They represented a fusion of congregation and community, a union of the sacred and the secular. In early days, as the Saints struggled to exist in a variety of hostile landscapes, the distinction between things secular and those sacred was necessarily blurred. The temporal and ecclesiastical affairs of the community were intermingled, and ward bishops often functioned both as secular and ecclesiastical leaders.

In our day the Mormon village has given way to the ward, as pointed out by Douglas Alder in his landmark study of the evolution and history of wards in the Church. Alder says: "The ward has become a less demanding but more expandable unit than the village. Instead of being agrarian like the village, the ward has become largely suburban as has the society in which it thrives. . . . Instead of promoting the organic unity of religion with economy, the ward is now the center of religious, social activities."

Alder's insightful comment that in the ward we see what Mormonism is bears repetition. In the ward, he says, "We will see a young person confessing sins in confidence to a bishop, youth leaders anguished about a rebellious youngster who defies principles—maybe even diverting a whole peer group—parents trying to moderate the competitiveness of a fourth grade age mate group, a teacher breaking through to a child where a parent cannot, adult loneliness crying out for someone to care, members of all ages giving talks—building fledgling confidence—councils and presidencies planning and worrying about members with personal difficulties, feelings of joy when someone makes solid decisions, gratefulness for life and for eternal purpose, a divorcee sitting with her four children and biting her lip through a Father's Day program, friends helping a mother cope with the shock when her child is born with imperfections, quorum members trying to help a father regain his church membership following transgression, vigils beside the dying, struggles for testimony, the exultant joy of belief, soul-searching before a mission call, concern about eternal progression, a couple trying to govern their courtship with traditional values, people struggling to pay tithing, newcomers who are anxious about acceptance when moving into the tight relationships of a new ward, temple attenders pondering the meaning of the endowment, a neighbor raising her hand to the square to support a ward division she really doesn't want, a mother deciding whether to accept an additional calling that seems to be one too many, members accepting the irritating personality of someone they would be tempted to ignore if he weren't a 'brother.' It is experiencing love—together."[23]

108

The sense of personal attachments to others remains a potent force in the Church today. No matter where one attends Church, whether in Logan, Lethbridge, Lagos, or London, it is a common experience to find someone at sacrament meeting, priesthood, or Relief Society whom we know, or who knows someone we know. With that sense of community, of belonging, comes a sense of caring for others and a commitment to them. I well recall when my wife and I and our two children, aged two years and six months, arrived in Ithaca, New York, in August 1953. We were recent converts to the Church. We knew no one in Ithaca, and we were in desperate need of a place to stay. We had almost no money. The local branch president and his wife welcomed us with open arms, provided us with a temporary place in their own home, and helped us to find more permanent quarters. A few years later, when our family, now grown to five children, arrived in Ottawa, Canada, we were invited to dinners, welcomed by branch leaders and members alike, and promptly called to Church positions where we could serve and learn with others.

We must not, however, be unaware of factors that in our day can tend to weaken the sense of community among the Saints. They include spiritual complacency in geographical areas of cultural homogeneity, a feeling that "all is well in Zion" and that "we have it made," the unwarranted notion that there is no urgency to reach out to others, particularly those not of our faith. With such complacency may come an unwillingness to accept people from other cultures, to consider them as "strangers and foreigners," rather than "fellowcitizens with the saints" (Ephesians 2:19). Yet a third danger is the increasing secularization of our society, with the attendant pressures for individuals and families to participate in a broad variety of experiences, from ballet lessons to Little League baseball. These may not, in and of themselves, be undesirable, but their cumulative effect may weaken the ties that bind the Saints together.

Other Factors in Building a Community of Saints

What then is involved in building a true community of believers? The factors noted by Stark—love and charity toward others, a shared faith springing from deeply held religious beliefs, a sense of community with associated deep personal attachments to others—obviously are important. But there are others as well. They include the following:

A sufficient proximity of members so they can "meet together often" (D&C 20:55) and serve each other, formally and informally (see Moroni 6:5–6). Of course, the proximity of members to each other varies significantly from one part of the world to another. Many wards in the Intermountain West of the United States are comprised of only a few city blocks, but when we returned to Ottawa, Canada, in 1959, we lived nearly an hour by automobile from our meeting place, and the nearest Church member in the suburban area in which we lived was over three miles away.

The importance of proximity is, of course, conditioned by the availability of adequate means of transportation and of telephones, which help to link members together. In West Africa, where almost none of the members have automobiles and where public transportation, especially on Sundays, is either nonexistent or too expensive for a whole family to use, the vast majority walk to church. That in effect limits the size of a branch or ward to the distance people can walk, a few miles to and from church. The ready availability of automobiles and good roads on which to travel means that most North American members can travel farther to church and still make out all right. Many travel quite long distances, and count themselves blessed to do so. The stake in which we lived for several years in eastern Canada was then 250 miles long and 250 miles wide, and some home and visiting teaching routes involved round trips of nearly 100 miles. I served there as a branch, ward, district, or stake officer over some twenty-five years and often used to joke that I went to work on Monday morning to rest up after the weekend!

A sufficient number of members, beyond a family, to provide the "critical mass" needed to operate Church programs. The average size of a ward has waxed and waned over time. Though a careful and prayerful decision is made in each instance, wards in the United States and Canada generally are considered for division nowadays when there are more than about 600 members. If wards become too large it is difficult to maintain a keen sense of community or to provide every member an opportunity to be involved in meaningful service to others.

Although the ward is the primary unit of the Latter-day Saint community, much smaller groups can also provide that essential sense of belonging. Because of where we lived in eastern Canada, our children were almost always numbered among the only two or three Latter-day Saints in their high schools. Their early-morning seminary class provided a sense of community for them. Each member of the class cared for, watched over, and worried about the others. If someone missed a morning's attendance, perhaps because of illness, there would be a telephone call within the hour from one or more of the others. The sense of belonging and of community was both real and reassuring.

A sufficient number of shepherds to lead, care for, and watch over the flock. Since the responsibility to provide leadership falls particularly on the priesthood, it is especially important there be sufficient active and able priesthood brethren to fulfill essential responsibilities.

111

A genuine identification with each other and a willingness to be known as members of The Church of Jesus Christ of Latter-day Saints, to be "fellowcitizens with the saints" (Ephesians 2:19), and "to be called [H]is people, [and be] willing to bear one another's burdens" (Mosiah 18:8).

A sufficient understanding of the gospel to comprehend the purpose of life. A community of believers can exist only if its members share an understanding of the doctrinal basis for their decisions and actions. These doctrines are found in the scriptures and in the teachings of the living prophets. They include faith in and a testimony of God the Eternal Father, in Jesus Christ, our Savior and Redeemer, and in the Holy Ghost, the testifier and Comforter; the plan of salvation, including the Atonement and Resurrection of Christ; priesthood and its keys; ordinances and covenants; continuing revelation; and the role of the prophet Joseph Smith in bringing to pass the purposes of God for His children. In the final analysis it is an agreement on doctrine that above all else provides the framework and basis for a solid, enduring community of believers.

A genuine determination to move steadily forward and to persevere regardless of external pressures, to endure to the end, to strive constantly to become of "one heart and one mind" (Moses 7:18), even the mind of Christ (see 1 Corinthians 2:16).

Insistence on the maintenance of high standards by Church members, in matters of both doctrine and behavior.

In their insightful work on religion in America, Roger Finke and Rodney Stark have developed a compelling argument for the proposition that "religious organizations are stronger to the degree that they impose significant costs in terms of sacrifice and even stigma upon their members."[24] In other words, the more comfortable the pew, the quicker the slide downhill.

Why do increased costs strengthen a community of believers? Finke and Stark suggest the following reasons:

- Prospective members are forced to choose whether they will participate fully or not at all. Potential members whose commitment and participation would otherwise be low are screened out. In Latter-day Saint parlance, members are required to put away "the natural man" and experience a "mighty change of heart" (see Mosiah 3:19; Alma 5:12–13).

- The social and spiritual rewards for displaying high levels of commitment are substantially increased.

- Success breeds success. Positive experiences in worship services increase to the degree that the church is full, members are enthusiastically participating, and the believers are giving a positive evaluation of what is going on.

How blessed we are that the Brethren stand as mighty watchmen on the tower, preaching both by precept and example the absolute need for all God's children to grow in faith, integrity, and righteousness. They call upon us to give away all of our sins, to overcome the natural man who is the enemy of God (see Alma 22:18), and to live *all* of Christ's commandments *all* of the time. Our willingness to do so is the measure of our devotion and commitment to Christ. These words of Jesus tell us of our duty, "He that hath my commandments, and keepeth them, he it is that loveth me: and he that loveth me shall be loved of my Father, and I will love him, and will manifest myself to him" (John 14:21).

As the secular communities in which many of us live continue to flag and falter, the Saints must be prepared to speak up with regard to public matters that are moral in nature and to vote for men and women who reflect our values. Note this wise counsel from President Gordon B. Hinckley: "The

113

building of public sentiment begins with a few earnest voices. I am not one to advocate shouting defiantly or shaking fists and issuing threats in the faces of legislators. But I am one who believes that we should earnestly and sincerely and positively express our convictions to those given the heavy responsibility of making and enforcing our laws. The sad fact is that the minority who call for greater liberalization, who peddle and devour pornography, who encourage and feed on licentious display make their voices heard until those in our legislatures may come to believe that what they say represents the will of the majority. We are not likely to get that which we do not speak up for."[25]

It will often be wise for us to lift our voices with those of others who feel as we do, to make common cause with other men and women of good will and anxious hearts who are concerned as we are concerned with what is wrong. These words of Edmund Burke come to mind, "When bad men combine, the good must associate; else they will fall, one by one, an unpitied sacrifice in a contemptible struggle."[26]

In addition to speaking up on moral issues, there is much more we can do, as citizens and as members of the community of Saints, to help make our neighborhoods better places in which to live. Service in the community might include working in such things as PTA, "Neighborhood Watch" programs, blood drives, Little League, etc. A few innovative examples of Christian service to others will illustrate the wide variety of other initiatives available to us as communities of Saints. They include the following:

◆ In an area of Salt Lake City where real poverty is not uncommon, a stake has embarked on an ambitious short-term plan to tutor junior high school students in English, science, and math. Their mid-range plan is to expand the tutoring to all students in need within the stake's boundaries, from kindergarten through high school. Long range, they intend to tutor the parents and family members of these students, with a special emphasis on basic literacy.

◆ Two different stakes in the Salt Lake City area approached their respective county commissioners and offered to build a public park; the Church would provide the labor if the municipalities would donate the land, provide heavy equipment, and commit to the aftercare. In one instance, a thirty-five-year rift between the stake and a neighboring congregation of another faith was healed as a consequence of the park project they worked on together. In the other instance, the stake and four non-LDS churches joined together to make the park a new community landmark.

◆ A student stake in Logan, Utah, laboriously tape records the contents of university textbooks each quarter so that disabled college students can study and perform their assignments.

With a little thought and a lot of effort, there is no end to what we can do to help strengthen our communities.

EPILOGUE

As President Howard W. Hunter has reminded us, "We are at a time in the history of the world and the growth of the Church when we must think more of holy things and act more like the Savior would expect his disciples to act."[1] The clouds of night's darkness are drawing in on a world drenched with wickedness and stained with sin.

In Proverbs we read, "For the commandment is a lamp" (Proverbs 6:23). In a world that pays increasingly less attention to Christ and His commandments, and is increasingly hostile to "the unsearchable riches of Christ" (Ephesians 3:8), the light of the commandments shines less brightly in many hearts and homes. Once the light is dimmed, individuals and society lose both their ability to distinguish between right and wrong and the will to act on what is right. Many are left to grope blindly in the darkness, knowing not where to turn, stumbling, losing their way, forever falling back.

Yet we should not despair but be filled with hope. There *is* a light in the darkness, even the light of the Savior of the world. "I am the light of the world," Jesus proclaimed. "He that followeth me shall not walk in darkness, but shall have the light of life" (John 8:12). He calls us "out of darkness into his marvellous light" (1 Peter 2:9). The "darkness is past, and the true light now shineth" (1 John 2:8).

117

The light shines most brightly in those who are "pure in heart," the Zion people of God. They are those whose eyes are "single to my glory," whose "whole bodies shall be filled with light, and there shall be no darkness in [them]" (D&C 88:67).

There is no doubt we will need to draw upon that light in the coming days. President Heber C. Kimball foresaw our time, I believe, when he said: "Let me say to you, that many of you will see the time when you will have all the trouble, trial and persecution that you can stand, and plenty of opportunities to show that you are true to God and his work. This Church has before it many close places through which it will have to pass before the work of God is crowned with victory. To meet the difficulties that are coming, it will be necessary for you to have a knowledge of the truth of this work for yourselves. The difficulties will be of such a character that the man or woman who does not possess this personal knowledge or witness will fall. If you have not got the testimony, live right and call upon the Lord and cease not till you obtain it. If you do not you will not stand.

"Remember these sayings, for many of you will live to see them fulfilled. The time will come when no man nor woman will be able to endure on borrowed light. Each will have to be guided by the light within himself. If you do not have it, how can you stand?"[2]

The light of growing numbers of the pure in heart joined together in families and in communities of believers fuses to form a mighty beacon, a light to all the world. Thus is Zion a light in the darkness, a refuge for the righteous, called to be so by the Savior himself: "Arise and shine forth, that thy light may be a standard for the nations; and that the gathering together upon the land of Zion, and upon her stakes, may be for a defense, and for a refuge from the storm, and from wrath when it shall be poured out without mixture upon the whole earth" (D&C 115:5–6). We are not only to look to the Light for guidance and strength, but we also have the solemn obligation to light the candles ourselves, each of us doing his or her part to dispel the darkness.

Only by turning away from the world to embrace the gospel of Jesus Christ and his Church can we find the personal and collective peace and safety so longed for and urgently required. If we are to roll back the darkness, which threatens to overwhelm our society, we must begin with the eternal task of transforming ourselves, cleansing the inner vessel, and simultaneously moving outward to strengthen our families and communities.

What is required of each aspiring disciple, I believe, is to rise above the casual, complacent, culturally-rooted commitment to Christ characteristic of too many who dare to call themselves Saints. We must become consumed by Christ, set spiritually afire by him, consecrated to his cause, completely committed to the work of the Kingdom, resolved to pay whatever demand of service or sacrifice he requires of us. Diligence and devotion must be our watchwords, endurance to the end our firm determination. When the prophets point the way, we must have the courage to follow.

It is said that every journey commences with a single step. Ours, by contrast, should begin with us on our knees, in humble supplication to the Source of truth and light. He will guide us. He knows the way. He has traveled the road before us. The price of knowing him, of following him, of becoming like him, is the same today as always. Simply put, we must give away all of our sins to know him. The demands of discipleship are at the same time both simple and difficult. God bless us and give us the courage to accept it, with all our hearts.

119

NOTES

Notes to Introduction

1. Alexander B. Morrison, *Visions of Zion* [1993], 1.
2. *Ensign*, June 1976, 4.
3. In *Journal of Discourses*, 20:135–36.
4. *Ensign*, November 1995, 72.
5. *Ensign*, May 1996, 83.
6. *Ensign*, November 1980, 51.

Notes to Chapter One

1. "Qualifying American's Decline," March 15, 1993, 12.
2. These statistics are taken except as noted otherwise from *The Index of Leading Cultural Indicators*, Volume 1, 1993, published jointly by The Heritage Foundation and Empower America.
3. Charles Murray, "The Coming White Underclass," *The Wall Street Journal*, October 29, 1993.
4. *Report to Congress on Out of Wedlock Childbearing*, DHHS, pub. 95–1257–1 [September 1995].
5. *The Salt Lake Tribune*, August 8, 1996, A-3.
6. U.S. Bureau of Labor Statistics, Bulletin 2307, 1994.
7. *Children's Defense Fund*, "Facts and Figures," 1996. Information obtained from CDF's home page on the World Wide Web.
8. *U.S. News and World Report*, January 17, 1994, 24.
9. *The Salt Lake Tribune*, August 21, 1995.
10. See *Preventing Teenage Pregnancy in Forsyth County*, William B. Hansen, Principal Investigator, Bowman Gray School of Medicine, Winston-Salem, N.C.

Notes to Chapter Two

1. The *California Children of Divorce Study*, directed by Judith Wallerstein, a noted social scientist; David van Biema, "The Price of a Broken Home," reported by Elizabeth B. Mullen, *Time*, February 27, 1995, 53.
2. "Child Abuse and Other Risks of Not Living with Both Parents," *Ethology and Sociobiology*, 6:197, 1985.
3. *The Atlantic Monthly*, April, 1993, 55–56.

4. *The Chronicle of Higher Education,* April 14, 1993.
5. Readers will note that in an earlier discussion (see p. 4) illegitimacy, not fatherlessness, was termed the most dangerous social trend of our time. Since the vast majority of illegitimate children are born into families with no father present, illegitimacy and fatherlessness are almost synonymous, at least in terms of their effects. See *Fatherless America: Confronting Our Most Urgent Social Problem,* BasicBooks, New York, 1995.
6. *Male and Female: A Study of the Sexes in a Changing World* [1969], 195.
7. See I. Garfinkel and S. S. McLanahan, *Single Mothers and Their Children,* Urban Institute, Washington, D.C., 1986, 30–31.
8. *Morbidity and Mortality Weekly Report,* March 4, 1994, 132–33.
9. U.S. Bureau of the Census, *Poverty in the United States: 1992,* Current Population Reports, Series P-60, no. 185, Table 4.121.

Notes to Chapter Three

1. The majority of the members of so-called "youth" gangs are actually adults. According to the 1995 report of the Salt Lake Area Gang Project, of the 3,104 identified gang members and associates in the Salt Lake Area, as of January 1, 1996, only 831 were juveniles.
2. *The State of America's Children Yearbook,* Children's Defense Fund [1995], 3.

Notes to Chapter Four

1. *Ensign,* October 1992, 69.
2. *American Mainline Religion: Its Changing Shape and Future* [1987], Chapter 2.
3. Charles Trueheart, "Welcome to the Next Church," *The Atlantic Monthly,* August 1996, 37.
4. H. Fairlie, *The Seven Deadly Sins Today* [1979], 113.
5. "A New Order of Religious Freedom," *First Things,* February 1992, 13.
6. *The New York Times Book Review,* February 7, 1993, 3.
7. William Bennett, *Imprimis,* 24, No. 11, November 1995, 5.
8. J. W. Hill, *Abraham Lincoln: Man of God* [1927], 391.

Notes to Chapter Five

1. *The Index of Leading Cultural Indicators,* ii.
2. James C. Humes, *The Wit & Wisdom of Winston Churchill* [1994], 114.
3. *First Things,* March 1994, 15–20.
4. *Men and Women of Christ* [1991], 9.
5. *Ensign,* May 1989, 4.
6. *Journal of Discourses* 21:3.
7. *Journal of Discourses* 3:15.

Notes to Chapter Six

1. William J. Bennett, *The Book of Virtues* [1993], 794–95.
2. Russ Walton, *Biblical Principles: Concerning Issues of Importance to Godly Christians* [1984], 361.
3. Quoted by Margaret Thatcher in *Imprimis,* 24, No. 3, March 1995, 1.

4. *Democracy in America* (Alfred A. Knopf, New York, 1980).
5. See *Church News*, March 9, 1996, 3.
6. *BYU Devotional and Fireside Speeches 1991–92*, 14 January 1992, 54.
7. *Ensign*, October 1992, 60.
8. See *Religion in America*, 1992–93, The Princeton Religion Research Center, Princeton, NJ, 1992–93, 25th Anniversary Edition, 23.
9. M. Novak, *Imprimis* 24, No. 5, May 1995, 6.
10. *Ensign*, October 1992, 62.
11. Quoted in Hadley Arkes, "Morality and the Law," *The Wilson Quarterly*, Spring 1981, 102.
12. *The Interaction of Law and Religion* [1974], 137–38.
13. Thomas G. West, *The Federalist Papers and the American Founding*, ed. Charles R. Kesler [1987], 166–67.
14. *Journal of Discourses* 12:111.
15. *Journal of Discourses* 12:109.
16. *Journal of Discourses* 21:2.
17. *Journal of Discourses* 24:176.
18. *Meek and Lowly*, [1987], ix, 3.
19. C. S. Lewis, *The Screwtape Letters* [1961], 56.

Notes to Chapter Seven

1. *Ensign*, November 1980, 4.
2. *Ensign*, November 1995, 102.
3. *The Teachings of Spencer W. Kimball* [1982], 315.
4. I am indebted to Professor Valerie Hudson of Brigham Young University for bringing this understanding to my attention.
5. *The Family: A Proclamation to the World*, *Ensign*, November 1995, 102.
6. *The Teachings of Spencer W. Kimball* [1982], 324.
7. *Ensign*, May 1980, 52.
8. *Ensign*, November 1995, 102.
9. *The Teachings of Spencer W. Kimball*, 319.
10. Address given to Seminary and Institute Faculty, at Brigham Young University, 15 July 1958.
11. *Ensign*, November 1986, 7.
12. *Ensign*, May 1978, 93.
13. *God, Family, Country: Our Three Great Loyalties* [1974], 196.
14. Conference Report, October 1945, 48.
15. "The Law of Chastity," *The New Era*, January 1988, 5.
16. *Ensign*, November 1990, 47.
17. *Ensign*, November 1993, 59.
18. J. David Hawkins, "Controlling Crime before It Happens: Risk-Focused Prevention," *National Institute of Justice Journal*, August 1995, 10–18.
19. See Salt Lake Area Gang Project, *Informant*, Fall, 1995, 1.
20. *Ensign*, November 1994, 49–51.
21. *Ensign*, May 1995, 67–68.
22. *Evidences and Reconciliations* [1943], 72.
23. *Ensign*, November 1995, 62; emphasis added.

Notes to Chapter Eight

1. The *Webster's New International Dictionary* (second ed., unabridged, G&C Merriam Company, Springfield, Mass., 1944).
2. In *Journal of Discourses* 17:75.
3. *The Northern Anthology of American Literature*, 2d ed. [1986], 14.
4. See *The Rise of Christianity: A Sociologist Reconsiders History* [1996].
5. See William H. McNeill, *Plagues and Peoples* [1976], 108–9.
6. See Stark, 82.
7. Ibid., 83–84.
8. Ibid., 87.
9. *Teachings of the Prophet Joseph Smith*, sel. Joseph Fielding Smith [1976], 178–79; emphasis added.
10. *Times and Seasons*, 3:732.
11. Kenneth W. Godfrey, Audrey M. Godfrey, Jill Mulvay Derr, *Women's Voices, An Untold History of the Latter-day Saints, 1830–1900* [1982], 238–39.
12. LeRoy R. Hafen and Ann W. Hafen, *Handcarts to Zion* [1960], 61.
13. Kate B. Carter, comp., *Treasures of Pioneer History*, vol. 5 [1956], 240–42.
14. *Handcarts to Zion*, 61.
15. McNeill, *Plagues and Peoples*, 108.
16. Stark, *The Rise of Christianity*, 81.
17. *Church News*, May 26, 1979, 4.
18. *The Rise of Christianity*, 161, 213.
19. Quoted by Leonard J. Arrington, "Planning an Iron Industry for Utah, 1851–1898," *Huntington Library Quarterly*, 21 [May 1958], 249.
20. In *Mormonism: A Faith for All Cultures* [1978], 9.
21. Ibid., 55–56.
22. It must be noted, however, that many early British converts to The Church of Jesus Christ of Latter-day Saints evidently *were* serious seekers of religious truth, unsatisfied with what they had and actively looking for more. Of course, many may have satisfied those desires through contacts with others who were either members or were themselves investigating the Church. (See Malcolm R. Throp, "The Religious Background of Mormon Converts in Britain, 1837–52," *Journal of Mormon History* 4:51, 1977.)
23. See "The Mormon Ward: Congregation or Community?" *Journal of Mormon History* 5:61–78, 1978.
24. *The Churching of America, 1776–1990: Winners and Losers in Our Religious Economy* [1992], 238–75.
25. *Ensign*, November 1975, 39.
26. *The Oxford Dictionary of Quotations* [1987], 108.

Notes to Epilogue

1. *Ensign*, November 1994, 87.
2. Orson F. Whitney, *The Life of Heber C. Kimball* [1992], 449–50.

BIBLIOGRAPHY

Alder, Douglas D. "The Mormon Ward: Congregation or Community?" *Journal of Mormon History*, vol. 5, 1978.

Arkes, Hadley "Morality and the Law," *The Wilson Quarterly*, Spring, 1981.

Arrington, Leonard J. "Planning an Iron Industry for Utah, 1851–1858," *Huntington Library Quarterly*, May, 1958.

Bennett, William J. "Redeeming Our Time," *Imprimis*, November, 1995.

_____. William J. *The Book of Virtues*. New York: Simon & Schuster, 1993.

_____. "Qualifying America's Decline," *Wall Street Journal*, March 15, 1993.

Benson, Ezra Taft. "Beware of Pride," *Ensign*, May 1989.

_____. "The Law of Chastity," *New Era*, January 1988.

_____. *God, Family, Country: Our Three Great Loyalties*. Salt Lake City: Deseret Book Co., 1974.

Berman, Harold J. *The Interaction of Law and Religion*. New York: Abingdon Press, 1974.

Blankenhorn, David. *Fatherless America: Confronting Our Most Urgent Social Problem*. New York: Basic Books, 1995.

Carter, Kate B., comp. *Treasures of Pioneer History*. Salt Lake City: Daughters of the Utah Pioneers, 1956.

Daly, Martin, and Wilson, Margo, "Child Abuse and Other Risks of Not Living with Both Parents," New York: *Department of Psychology, McMaster University, 1985.*

Dawson, Deborah A. "Family Structure and Children's Health and Well-being," *Journal of Marriage & the Family*, August 1991.

Faust, James E. "A New Civil Religion," *Ensign*, October 1992.

Finke, Roger, and Rodney Stark, *The Churching of America, 1776–1990*. New Brunswick: Rutgers University Press, 1992.

First Presidency and Council of the Twelve Apostles. *The Family: A Proclamation to the World. Ensign*, November 1995.

Garfinkel, Irwin, and McLanahan, Sara S. *Single Mothers and Their Children: A New American Dilemma*. Washington, D.C.: The Urban Institute Press, 1986.

Godfrey, Kenneth W., Audrey M. Godfrey, and Jill Mulvay Derr. *Women's Voices: An Untold History of the Latter-day Saints, 1830–1900*. Salt Lake City: Deseret Book Co., 1982.

Hafen, LeRoy R., and Ann W. Hafen. *Handcarts to Zion*. Glendale: The Arthur H. Clark Co., 1960.

Hansen, William B. *Preventing Teenage Pregnancy in Forsyth County*, Winston-Salem, N.C.: Bowman Gray School of Medicine, Wake Forest University, 1990.

Hawkins, J. David. "Controlling Crime before It Happens: Risk-Focused Prevention," *National Institute of Justice Journal*, August 1995.

Hill, John Wesley. *Abraham Lincoln: Man of God*. New York: G.P. Putnam's Sons, 1927.

Hinckley, Gordon B. "Bring Up a Child in the Way He Should Go," *Ensign*, November 1993.

———. "Opposing Evil," *Ensign*, November 1975.

———. Save the Children," *Ensign*, November, 1994.

Humes, James C. *The Wit and Wisdom of Winston Churchill*. New York: HarperCollins Publishers, 1978.

Hunter, Howard W. "Being a Righteous Husband and Father," *Ensign*, November 1994.

———. "Follow the Son of God," *Ensign*, November 1994.

Journal of Discourses. 26 vols. London: Latter-day Saints' Book Depot, 1854–1886. Vols. 3, 12, 17, 20, 21, 24.

Kimball, Edward L., ed. *The Teachings of Spencer W. Kimball*. Salt Lake City: Bookcraft, 1982.

Kimball, Spencer W. "Families Can Be Eternal," *Ensign*, November 1980.

———. "The False Gods We Worship," *Ensign*, June 1976.

Lee, Harold B. "Testimony." In *Conference Report*. Salt Lake City: The Church of Jesus Christ of Latter-day Saints, October 1971.

Lee, Rex E. "Things That Change, And Things That Don't," *Devotional Speeches of the Year*. Provo, Utah: Brigham Young University Press, 1992.

Lewis, C.S. *The Screwtape Letters*. New York: Collier Books, 1961.

Lloyd, R. Scott, "Lady Thatcher Sees LDS British Influence," *Church News*, March 9, 1996.

Maxwell, Neal A. "Deny Yourselves of All Ungodliness," *Ensign*, May 1995.

———. *Meek and Lowly*. Salt Lake City: Deseret Book Co., 1987.

———. *Men and Women of Christ*. Salt Lake City: Bookcraft, 1991.

McCullough, Marie. "On Chastity, Teens Practice What Mothers Preach," *The Salt Lake Tribune*, August 14, 1996.

McKay, David O. In *Conference Report*, October 1958

McNeill, William H. *Plagues and Peoples*. Garden City: Anchor Books, 1976.

Mead, Margaret. *Male and Female: A Study of the Sexes in a Changing World*. New York: William Morrow & Co., 1949.

Monson, Thomas S. "That We May Touch Heaven," *Ensign*, November 1990.

Morrison, Alexander B. *Visions of Zion*. Salt Lake City, Utah: Deseret Book, 1993.

Murray, Charles. "The Coming White Underclass," *The Wall Street Journal*, Friday, October 29, 1993.

Neuhaus, Richard John. "A New Order of Religious Freedom," *First Things: A Monthly Journal of Religion and Public Life*, February 1992.

Novak, Michael. "A New Vision of Man," *Imprimis*, May 1995.

Bezilla, Robert, ed. "Religion in America: 1992–1993." Princeton: Princeton Religion Research Center, 1994.

Oaks, Dallin H. "Religious Values and Public Policy," *Ensign*, October 1992.

Packer, Boyd K. "Little Children," *Ensign*, November 1986.

———. "Solving Emotional Problems in the Lord's Own Way," *Ensign*, May 1978.

———. "The Father and the Family," *Ensign*, May 1994.

Smith, Joseph. *History of the Church*. 7 vols. Salt Lake City: Deseret Book.

———. *Teachings of the Prophet Joseph Smith*. comp. Joseph Fielding Smith. Salt Lake City: Deseret Book Co., 1976.

Solzhenitsyn, Aleksandr. "The Relentless Cult of Novelty and How It Wrecked the Century," *The New York Times Book Review*, February 7, 1993.

Stark, Rodney. *The Rise of Christianity*. Princeton: Princeton University Press, 1996.

Thatcher, Margaret. "The Moral Foundations of Society," *Imprimis*, March 1995.

"The State of America's Children Yearbook," *Children's Defense Fund*, 1995.

Thorp, Malcolm R. "The Religious Backgrounds of Mormon Converts in Britain, 1837–52," *Journal of Mormon History*, vol. 4, 1977.

Tullis, F. LaMond, ed. *Mormonism: A Faith for All Cultures*. Provo: Brigham Young University Press, 1978.

U.S. Bureau of the Census. *Statistical Abstract of the United States: 1995* (115th edition). Washington, DC, 1995.

Van Orden, Dell. "Members Answer Calls to Colonize Despite Hardships," *Church News*, May 26, 1979.

Wade, Clark Roof, and William McKinney. *American Mainline Religion*, New Brunswick: Rutgers University Press, 1987.

Walton, Russ. *Biblical Principles: Concerning Issues of Importance to Godly Christians*. Plymouth, Mass.: Plymouth Rock Foundation, 1984.

West, Thomas G. *The Federalist Papers and the American Founding*, Charles R. Kesler, ed. New York: The Free Press, 1987.

"What Do Gang Members Say about Prevention?" *Salt Lake Area Gang Project Informant*, Fall 1995.

Whitehead, Barbara Dafoe. "Dan Quayle Was Right," *The Atlantic Monthly*, April 1993.

Whitney, Orson F. *The Life of Heber C. Kimball*. Salt Lake City: Bookcraft, 1945.

Winthrop, John. "A Model of Christian Charity," *The Norton Anthology of American Literature*. New York: W.W. Norton & Co., 1986.

127

INDEX

Literacy effort, example of, 114–15
Loader, Patience, 99–100
Los Angeles riots, 38
Love: among Zion people, 71; teens need, 79; dies as result of immorality, 81; Christian community shows, 97–98; Mormon pioneers show, 98–102
Loyalty to gang, 20, 27

Madison, James, 50
Mafia, 20
Marriage: reduces frequency of domestic violence, 17; sexual indulgence diminishes sanctity of, 42; importance of, 69–73, 88–89; equality in, 70, 90, 91
Martin Handcart Company, 99–100
Maxwell, Neal A.: on selfishness, 43; on meekness, 65–66; on sacrificing the animal within us, 91
McArthur Handcart Company, 100–102
McConkie, Bruce R., xii–xiii
McNeill, William H., 102–3
Mead, Margaret, 16
Media: respect for religion portrayed in, 32; promotes violence, 84
Meekness, 65–66
Men, fatherhood benefits, 16, 18, 91. See also Fathers
Mentors, teens need adult, 79, 86, 87–88
Mercy, 58–59
Miller, Ruben, 104
Missionary work, 77, 107
Mitchum, Robert, 32
Monson, Thomas S., 81
Moral absolutes versus moral relativism, 55–57
Morality: must be based on religious principles, 49–51; speaking up for, 57, 113–14; private and public, 59, 67–68
Mothers: unwed, 4–5, 7, 16–17; working outside home, 6,

73–74; have complementary role in family, 89–90
Movies. See Media

Natural man, 43, 65, 70, 91, 113
Networking brings religious conversion, 106–7
Neuhaus, Richard John, 37

Oaks, Dallin H.: on moral absolutes v. moral relativism, 55–56; on standing up for values, 57
Optimism, xii

Packer, Boyd K.: on mothers needed at home, 73–74; on improving behavior, 74; on responsibility of parents, 75
Parable: of the sower, 39, 65; of the good Samaritan, 54–55
Parents: link past and future, 70; duty of, to rear children, 71–74; responsible to teach youth, 74–75, 79–80; need to show love, 79; should meet children's friends, 82; control risk factors for violent behavior, 83–84; gang members express expectations about, 87; as leaders in family, 91. See also Fathers; Mothers
Park, example of building public, 115
Parker, Ada, 101
Parker, Ann, 100–102
Parker, Arthur, 100–102
Parker, Martha Alice, 101
Parker, Max, 101
Parker, Robert, 100–102
Paul the apostle, 63–65
Peace, Zion as place of, ix–xiii
Peer groups, 86. See also Friends
Pessimism about American future, 36
Pioneers: handcart, show compassion, 98–102; colonize Intermountain West, 103–5, 107
Plagues, 97–98, 103